Your Life Matters!

8 Simple Steps to Writing Your Story

JUNIE SWADRON

NEW YORK

LONDON • NASHVILLE • MELBOURNE • VANCOUVER

Your Life Matters!
8 Simple Steps to Writing Your Story

Published in New York, New York, by Morgan James Publishing in partnership with Difference Press. Morgan James is a trademark of Morgan James, LLC. www.MorganJamesPublishing.com

ISBN 978-1-64279-951-4 paperback
ISBN 978-1-64279-952-1 eBook
Library of Congress Control Number: 2019919806

Cover Design Concept:
Nakita Duncan

Cover Design by:
Rachel Lopez
www.r2cdesign.com

Interior Design by:
Bonnie Bushman
The Whole Caboodle Graphic Design

Editor:
Cory Hott

Book Coaching:
The Author Incubator

Morgan James is a proud partner of Habitat for Humanity Peninsula and Greater Williamsburg. Partners in building since 2006.

Get involved today! Visit
www.MorganJamesBuilds.com

Without the presence of God's love in my life, I cannot fathom where I might be today. The unmistakable benevolence that holds me in my darkest hour, and the unimaginable joy that fills me when inspiration hits, are beyond description. Between the extremes of despair and elation is the place where I rest knowing the Source of Infinite Love is available to me in every moment. For this I am eternally grateful.

I dedicate this book to my fellow elders who have been on the planet for more than sixty years and are ready to celebrate their life journey through the sacred stories they can tell and teach. I honour you. And to my late mother, Minnie Swadron, who said, "Junie, you are never old when you are happy."

And whatever your age, if you are reading these words, I also dedicate this book to you, because your life matters and the stories you have lived are worth telling.

"The sweet whisperings of your soul meet you on the page and something shifts. You strengthen. You begin to stand taller and one day you notice that your voice on the page has become your voice in the world."

Junie Swadron

Table of Contents

Foreword

Those words by Byron Katie were on my fridge door for years. They always seemed to soothe my soul when it was troubled and restless. Those words also reminded me of a book I read many years ago called *All Sickness is Homesickness*. I think that our longing to go home is one of the most profound longings we have as humans. But where is home and what is it? Katie's quote suggests that home resides within us— internally, not externally. But what if that which resides internally, at a subconscious level, is not a happy place? A place we want to run from rather than run to? Then home is not where we want to be for very long. What if we could make our "inner world" a happier place to reside? It wasn't until now, while writing this foreword, that the answer found me—one of those wonderful "Aha!" moments that can change your life in a heartbeat.

This book, *Your Life Matters: 8 Simple Steps to Writing Your Story* by Junie Swadron, could be the answer. What if I could feel at home with my past experiences and enjoy the person I've become over the years? What if I could rewrite my life as a way to purge my past? And what if I could celebrate the wisdom I have gleaned over my lifetime?

The good news is that I can because that's exactly what Junie did. In spite of being diagnosed in 1969 at the age of twenty with manic depressive illness, she rose above the challenges that were destroying her life and a big part of her healing journey was through writing. I have done the same. Like Junie, I've kept a journal since my early twenties. It has always been a safe refuge, a place where I could talk things through and, in so doing, find solace. Even though I like to write in my journal, I never thought I would write my memoir. Now, I'm ready because the book you're holding is going to make it possible in eight easy steps. All I need is the willingness to begin the process of opening my heart and my mind to the possibility that I can do it. As Junie says, "You don't need fancy language or anything other than a willingness to tell the truth as you remember it."

I would never have been as motivated as I am now if I hadn't made the connection between my longing for home and my ability to get there by writing my memoir. If all sickness is really homesickness, then imagine how many patients could heal themselves of their illness. Imagine if doctors prescribed a journal and a pen for their patients instead of a drug. There are side effects for both, but the side effects of pharmaceuticals are often negative, while the side effects of journaling often lead to tranquility, healing, and self-discovery.

Imagine if this book was in all the doctors' offices around the country and in all the hospitals. Imagine. Patients could listen to this as an audio book instead of watching sitcoms to numb their pain. I first met Junie at the Imagine Cafe in Victoria, British Columbia, Canada at her book launch for *Write Where You Are*. In addition to being a writer, she is also a psychotherapist. But what particularly intrigued me was the fact that she has bipolar illness and knows both sides of the couch. Her credentials were impressive as an author, speaker, psychotherapist, workshop facilitator, and professional coach, but that's not what drew me to her. It was her gentleness and vulnerability that touched me to the core.

She writes, "I started out as a frightened child and used my journal as a way to release my pain. Many of my entries would, unwittingly, turn into poems, short stories and songs. It led me down a path where my journal became my best friend. It was always available to hold me, comfort me and allow my creativity to emerge on the page. I could tell it all my secrets. Eventually, I gained self-confidence. I began to allow myself to be seen and heard. To love myself more, to practice self-compassion. Eventually I was standing taller and sharing my creativity that I had been too ashamed to do in the past. My voice on the page was becoming my voice in the world. In conversations, in books, in classes, in talks."

Junie's book teaches us that we can accomplish this, too.

In Brenda Ueland's classic book, *If You Want to Write*, she advises to write because you want to tell the truth, not because you want to be famous or a published author. When we speak and write the truth, we come to believe that our thoughts matter. That we matter.

That our life matters. Oprah realized this after twenty-five years of interviewing people. She learned that the three things they all had in common was their need to be seen, heard, and know that what they thought mattered. Writing our memoir empowers us because we acknowledge that we matter—yet the crucial ingredient is courage.

If we still suffer from "the disease to please," it's unlikely we'll be willing to tell the truth lest we hurt someone's feelings or worse, make them angry. I find it still happens to me with my older sister. I still find myself deferring to her wishes. I should know better, but childhood conditioning is hard to undo. The other thing that I find difficult to do is silence the inner critic who asks the inevitable nasty questions, "So who do you think you are to be writing your memoir? Do you think your life is that interesting? Do you think anyone would care?" That unrelenting voice can harass me until I finally say, "Stop! I interrupt this broadcast for an important announcement! I am a child of the Universe and I deserve to follow my dream to write my memoir. My life matters!" And so does yours.

I wrote many more pages in this foreword that you don't need to read because they are the words of famous people that I have hidden behind. My daughter once said to me, "Mom, you're always quoting other people. I'm not interested in what they think, I want to know what you think." After reading this foreword, Junie said the same thing. "Brigitte, you're still sounding like a victim, not like the accomplished woman I know you to be. I want to hear about your experiences. I want to know how your beautiful vulnerability has become your strength. Would you be willing to use that as a writing prompt to uncover the truth of who you are?"

I agreed, and wrote from my heart. Several hours later of uninterrupted writing turned my perceived weaknesses into strengths that I now recognize as having served me well throughout my life and my career as an educator and passion diviner. Being shamed as "too sensitive" served me well as a special education teacher and a guidance counsellor. I helped many students who were labelled as disabled to see themselves as gifted. Being shamed for having too much fantasy led to my career as a drama teacher. One of my dreams is to empower women of the world to live their dreams, regardless of their current reality.

The first step in accomplishing this is to believe that they matter. That their life matters. Both the pleasure and the pain of aging is that we get to reflect upon our life. Some parts bring us joy and other parts bring us sorrow and regret. Some experiences we'd like to relive and others we wish had never happened. But all make us who we are today and that is cause for celebration.

We're still alive to tell the tale. We all have a tale to tell but we're not all storytellers. The fact that you're reading this book suggests that you may be one of them. I encourage you to write your tale with the help of this book and perhaps with the help of Junie as your personal writing coach. You're worth it because your life matters!

Brigitte Rathje-Papadakis, M.A.,
Victoria, British Columbia, Canada

Chapter 1

This Is Your Life

Hello, beautiful reader. My heart welcomes you here, ready and excited to teach you what I have come to know on how to write life stories—to be the scribe, the author of the adventures you have lived. You will look back in time with the eyes of a compassionate witness to all you have experienced in your life. As well as living your life fully in today, you will look back in time with a curious and compassionate heart, opening to what you remember, observing from a place of spaciousness and from the loves and losses of your life.

It is a stunning experience to step back, breathe, and take a good look at this living masterpiece—your life—from the age you are today and notice whom you have become and notice, too, the myriad ways you became who you are.

This is you, honouring the magnificent life you have lived. You may feel trepidation, but my guess is that there is also exaltation because my words resonate with the truth of where you are right now. And because you are ready to write your memoir or special stories from your life journey even if you don't know how to go about it or where to begin. You may be scared of the entire process or have thoughts that say, "Who am I to write a book? Who would read it and, if they did, what would they think of me then?" You may even have specific people in mind—people close to you—whose opinions still matter the most, and you cringe at the thought of being judged.

I once received a fortune cookie that said, "Look for the dream that keeps coming back. It's your destiny." I kept it on my vision board for a long time, and then I wrote my first book because it was a dream that kept coming back.

If you have a dream to write your memoir or particular stories that you wish to record and it keeps coming back to you, it is not an accident. It is your destiny and I know that you know in your heart the truth of this. Dreams of the heart are God's first indication pointing you towards an open door where the manifestation of your dream awaits you. The door is never locked. In fact, it opens wide once you value yourself more than anyone else ever could. You do this by being caring and compassionate with the parts of you that don't believe you are bright enough, smart enough or have anything valuable to say. You must move beyond the voice of your inner critic that tells you that you might say things that are wrong, that you would appear stupid, or that no one would listen to your words, thoughts, and opinions. By doing this, you will come to remember who you really are and that you are worthy—that you matter—simply because you are here.

And that God, the Universe, wouldn't give you promptings to write your memoir if there wasn't substance to it.

You wouldn't be sitting up at night fretting over what you will do with your senior years. In fact, it frightens you as you approach the latter years of your life without knowing what you can do that will give it meaning—give you meaning. Who will you be without your career, a place to go to every day that not only gave you a routine but was also your identity?

Does this describe where you are right now? Your job, what you engaged in every day for years, is about to end or has already ended and you are troubled. Do you fall into bed at night feeling stressed because of the uncertainty that lies ahead? Perhaps you are concerned about your aging parents and imminent decisions about their fate or your adult children, praying they will make healthy choices so that their lives aren't burdened. Yet the biggest worry of all is wondering just what you will do with the rest of your life. Who will you be without your career, without somewhere to go when you wake up in the morning? How will you still contribute and feel needed and valued?

Or are you an entrepreneur who has overcome particular challenges and now offer your wisdom to others with your programs and services? And are willing to put *yoursef* into the story so your readers can trust you. They know you have gone the distance first-hand from your own unique experience – not just offering what you've read in a text book somewhere. And you also know writing a book will not only give you additional credibility, it allows you to reach unlimited numbers of people who can learn, grow and transform from your teachings.

The truth is—no matter what your age, senior or not—you wouldn't have an inner beckoning that doesn't quit telling you to share the incredible stories you have already lived in the form of a book if you weren't ready to do just that. Our inner promptings are not random. They are personal, a direct memo from the Universe into the inbox of our heart and soul and are meant for us to pay attention. Not someday. Today.

Do you say things like, "I've always been a good writer, or at least, I like to write and words just flow out of me when I journal—and I have dozens of them—or when I write letters, which I still love to do. In fact, when I do write, I forget about everything and everyone else. Time goes by magically, and I'm shocked to see how quickly. In fact, hours can slip by in minutes because I am fully present."

You are not alone. I know how that felt for me. Yet I was fifty years old before I was willing to go naked and tell my story. It was a huge leap, and I was willing to risk everything rather than continue to wear the masks that kept me in hiding. Yup, it was crazy—or was it?

> *"And the day came when the risk to remain tight in a bud was more painful than the risk it took to blossom."*
> **– Anaïs Nin**

If you are someone who wants to write your memoir and tell your stories because you would like to share what you have learned in order to make it just a wee bit easier for someone else who is travelling in the same moccasins that you have walked in, you know in your heart that you are meant to be reading these words right now. It's your calling, and it can be your destiny.

As well, if you want to write your memoir to leave a legacy to your children and grandchildren of what you have lived, what you have come to know for sure, and what has mattered most to you then you are in the right place.

Whatever your reasons, as you look back, write and reflect, you will learn things about yourself that you had not consciously realized before. One cannot look back without finding true hidden gems.

And it is worth every bit of trepidation and fear you might be having at the same time. Everyone I know who has ever written a memoir with me will tell you it is a scary proposition. One client, Doris, said, "I feel like my mouth and my throat are constipated, I am so scared." This changed as she continued to write fear-ward and forward. It always does.

When my clients move into the rhythm of their heart and stop listening to their harsh inner critic, they declare it was worth every word, every tear, every exhilaration. Why? Because they learn for themselves, through the process of scribing their stories, using my formula, the truth of these words: "The sweet whisperings of your soul meet you on the page and something shifts. You strengthen. You begin to stand taller and one day you notice that your voice on the page has become your voice in the world."

Hasn't every large transition in your life, as you stood at the precipice of change, frightened you? You wondered how you would get through it. You had sleepless nights. Yet you did get through it. Perhaps because you are stronger than you give yourself credit for.

Retirement doesn't mean what it meant years ago. You got your gold watch and don't have much now to look forward to or many years left to live past age sixty-five—the average retirement age. People are living ten, twenty, even thirty years longer these days and have the opportunity to make choices that truly matter to them.

At this stage, you are no longer burdened by what other people think you should be doing. You get to choose from your deepest truth. And when you do, there is nothing more liberating.

The same goes no matter what age you are and what stories you wish to tell to honour yourself and bring your light to others.

To not follow through on a dream that you secretly hold in your heart, to not stand up and learn to love and value your life when the opportunity knocks—especially when it's a truth, a desire, a dream that keeps returning to you, again and again—is a travesty.

Seriously. Life is not just a place to hang out between birth and death with a whole lot of movement or drama in between. It's something to be valued, honoured, and cherished. Breath is life and to have life is to have the living, breathing essence of God within our cells. It is a privilege that we must not take for granted. And our gift back to God for giving us this life is to live the best life we can live.

We all are products of our environment. We all are until we become conscious of the choices we are making. If you are still behaving out of beliefs you took on when you were a youngster, then it's time to ask yourself how well they serve you. If you say, "not well," then are you willing to become part of the club of awesome folk living life to the fullest?

There are so many things you have learned along life's journey and if you don't stop long enough to take stock of what they are, to truly find the courage to love yourself, there's a good chance you could die with your songs still buried inside you. And until that final breath, you will feel unfulfilled, live in a place of longing and envy, resenting the passing of days and years going by without making your dreams come true.

And unfortunately, there are countless elders and younger people, too, who feel that way right now. They are feeling old and used up. If you are of retirement age, are you afraid of being cast aside and becoming invisible to the eyes of the young? Feeling you no longer have anything to contribute? Do you believe society devalues the elderly? Is that true? It's only true if you believe it because then your life will reflect just that. If you believe you are fabulous, then the world you will experience will see you that way, too.

It's my aim to show you that you are. That you have a life worth celebrating and honouring and your dream to write your memoir is not simply possible and attainable—it's also easy. I know it because I've written books about writing as well as re-writing your life in order to let go of the painful past. This overlaps with what I'm talking about here.

Your sixties and beyond could be absolutely fabulous. That's what you can expect as you embrace your magnificence, know what you are capable of, and move into these next chapters of your life with confidence and verve.

It always excites me to show people how to write in such a way that their inner wisdom shows up on the page. You know your life, and you know what you have lived. You don't need fancy language or anything other than the willingness to tell the truth as you remember it. To show up and allow the writing to come forth effortlessly, which it will, when you align with what it is you wish to say. You will start to have newfound energy that you haven't seen in years—why? Because you are living your dream. You are putting pen to paper or fingers to keyboard. You are doing it just like you have done so many other things in your life.

Begin to remember all the projects or ways you have chosen to show up in the world, that would advance your life and help others as well. Think about what your friends and family admire about you? Think about your life challenges and how you got through them. What are your resilient tools—the ones you can teach others through what you have learned? Don't keep these to yourself. Just like the people who have been mentors to you along your life's journey, you can be that for others by not keeping your secrets buried. Your life stories are a treasure trove for you to explore. You will learn things about yourself you may not even have ever known because writing has a way about it that reveals insights and truths unnoticed by you beforehand.

As humans, the one constant we can rely on is change. Sometimes we sail merrily, merrily, merrily down the stream and life is but a dream, and other times, we don't know how we will survive the rapids. But dear reader, somehow, you did. And, somehow, I did too. And we meet here at this intersection because we have called each other in. The Universe brought us together so that you would be the answer to my dream—to write a book that melts your fears and doubts about writing your memoir by sharing what I have come to know about writing, about flow, about resistance, and about allowing.

Among the many directives of how to write a memoir, I have inserted some of my own life stories as examples that may inspire you; this book is not just a "how to," falling into the "no-no" rule in writing that says, "Show, don't tell." Instead, I will show you some of my stories—some in their rawest form, because this is memoir and it is written the way I remember it, not glossed over to sound pretty and poetic so that you will like me better.

As you move through the pages of this book, I wish to be your invisible, kind, and loving witness while you revisit and embrace the milestones that have made your life rich with meaning, the challenging and painful times, as well as the exciting and joyful ones. You will bring new clarity and understanding to old circumstances, put closure on unfinished business, laugh and cry at the meanderings of your life, and bring to the present new respect and reverence for the blessings of every day.

If you are standing on a precipice right now, but feel frozen, what will it cost you to make the decision to not write your memoir, to not bring you your dream come true?

Chapter 2

Let Me Introduce
Myself to You

When I was thirteen years old, I was given a diary for my birthday. I treasured that little red book with its tiny lock and key. It brought me into a private world no one else was allowed to enter. It sent me on a path of writing and healing that I would never have known back then. That writing became my panacea— the healing tool I would use throughout my life and also become the bedrock of my career. That diary became my best friend, my steady companion. I learned I could say things to it that I couldn't tell anyone else. I would write my secrets, my pain, my poetry, just about everything. In fact, my "diary", which I have since called my "journal", has provided me a safe refuge all through my life.

It never complains or gets bored or angry. I don't have to show up with my hair brushed, makeup on, clothes all clean and pressed. I can go to it in my pajamas or bring it to my favourite café or write in it in my doctor's office while waiting to be seen. There are no rules; just show up, pen in hand and a willingness to open to whatever comes.

Each of us defines success differently. For me, it meant being willing to go naked, to be vulnerable, and to find role models in books, coaches, therapists, teachers, and workshops that would teach me the tools I needed to unleash myself from my painful past and lead me to a high road towards a future that I would be proud of. And today I do stand proud. Not in an egotistic way, but in a way that I can say to you with every ounce of honesty and integrity, I have gone the distance and feel completely confident that if your dream is to write your memoir, to honour your life in ways you may not have thought of, I can guide you there in the eight easy steps that this book outlines.

When I was only twenty-eight, the first time I started to write down my life stories, feeling I had already lived extraordinary experiences, it felt right to start at the beginning. I wanted to unwrap the many traumatic situations that had occurred so I could heal and move on. I knew writing was the vehicle to get me there.

With the intention to hurt no one, I dug deep into my own psyche to bring back the essence of who I was. I wrote always with this question in mind, "What events took place that would shape and inform who I would become?"

I wrote chronologically, from my birth, forward. Later, however, I felt I needed to write stories that jumped out at me, even if they were no longer in order. I found that to be the best way because I could put them into their correct timeline later. I've since developed a system, which is the one in this book, but at that time, it was pure trial and error.

The one factor that has stood the test of time is that when I just wrote into the truth—not denying, embellishing, or quitting, just letting the pen have its way with me—the benefits were worth every unpleasant remembrance

However, there were also times I didn't write. Not at all. I didn't partake in its incredible generosity to help me find the answers that would give me the stability and clarity I needed. I called it writer's block, but what it really was, was fear. Fear of saying things I didn't want to hear—afraid to see them in print. I didn't want to hurt anyone. I was afraid to reveal things that I had kept secret for years.

Still I found myself sitting at my desk and starting one day. It came to the point that writing my life story was no longer an arbitrary choice. It was the healing vehicle that jumped out at me and I had to do it. My past was filled with so much pain that I knew if I didn't address it, it would eventually destroy me. I would continue to make poor choices, stay in unhealthy relationships, and be stuck in the loop of blame, shame, and depression. I knew I had to write my stories in order to claim back my life.

And so I did. With determination and patience I, as the older woman, was able to go back with a brand-new appreciation for all the different stages of who I—the infant, toddler, preteen, teenager, and younger adult—had once been. Looking back, I could see and feel her sadness, confusion, shyness, defensiveness, passion, joy, loves, and losses. Stepping outside and being a witness to my younger self, I got to know her in a way I had never known her before. I watched her in her unfolding and was able to bring to the younger me understanding, compassion, and forgiveness. The process taught me how to love myself.

On the pages I didn't have to play the roles I would sometimes play in the outside world. I didn't have to smile when I felt sad or be brave when I felt anything but courageous. I didn't have to be nice or unkind. I simply had to tell my truth.

It was in that process that I moved from loss and confusion into a place where things began to make sense, where clarity rose up from murky waters.

Over time I could see a palpable difference in the way I walked, the way I talked and the way I viewed the world. I became stronger, more confident and less afraid. I still had doubts and insecurities, but I was visibly miles ahead of where I had been before.

I learned at a young age how important our stories are, as they not only reflect the life journey we are on but also the events and circumstances that have shaped us and the decisions we made from the myriad choices available. Why did we choose this path over that one and what inspires us to move in the directions we do? It is complex, and there are so many reasons.

It was my natural curiosity and ability to see and hear what isn't always obvious to another that brought me to the work I do as both a psychotherapist and writing coach. My greatest joy is to inspire others to live the lives of their dreams. For some it could simply mean dreams of today.

When a person is afraid and lives with anxiety or depression, just walking outside the front door could be a huge triumph. In my counseling practice, I teach practical tools that foster hope and confidence. As my clients transform the pain of their past, many wish to write about their success. As a writing mentor, I guide them to find their voice on the page, which eventually becomes their voice in the world—both in their communication with others and, as I stated earlier, through books they write and often publish.

When I wrote my first book, *Re-Write Your Life: A Transformational Guide to Writing and Healing the Stories of Our Lives* in 2009, I came to the story, "A Time I Was Stronger Than I Thought." I wrote about my play, *Madness, Masks and Miracles*, and the backstory behind it and how it was the most challenging time of my life up to that point.

Yet I knew the play had to go on because it stopped being about me. It was about the message that had to be heard to help dispel myths and stigmas about mental illness. The courage I derived to actually stay with it came from Julia Cameron's famous book *The Artist's Way*. I facilitated a support group using that book for fifteen years, and it was the processes within it that gave me the impetus to write the play and song lyrics, act in it, and co-produce it.

It occurred to me while I wrote my book some years later that perhaps Julia Cameron would give me an endorsement. I hardly formed the thought in my head when a louder, nastier voice strode in and shouted in my ear, "Seriously? Who do you think you are? Why would she give *you* an endorsement? You've never written a book before. She wouldn't know you from Adam. She's a famous person," and on and on that relentless voice went, trying to drown out my inspiration. But I chose not to let it. Instead, I stood up for myself and responded, "Well, how do I know all that if I don't ask?"

I did, and to my amazing surprise, even though her publisher told me she didn't give endorsements anymore, she invited me to write her a letter anyway to ask her if she would. I did write one, and the next thing I knew, I was invited to send Julia Cameron my manuscript. Two weeks later, on my sixtieth birthday, I received the following endorsement:

"June Swadron is both a guide and a muse. Her book is a bright lantern, illuminating the often dark and tricky terrain of the soul. Grounded in personal experience, her techniques catalyze the deep authenticity possible to us all."

Thank goodness I didn't listen to my critical voice, or I never would have received an endorsement from a woman I so admired.

As you can imagine, I was over the moon. It is my honour to guide you into having the same kind of confidence while writing your life stories—to find the voice that may have been stolen from you since childhood. To not let nasty voices in your head stop you ever again from following your heart and living your dreams.

I love my work because I get to hear the enthusiasm and joy that comes from people who have worked with me:

- "I can do this."
- "I AM a writer."
- "I love what I have written."
- "I can't believe that just came out of my pen."
- "I feel so much better."
- "I have so much more clarity."
- "I have a direction."
- "My life does matter."
- "I've written my story. Yippee!"

Mostly I hear, "Thank you."

You never know who is going to read your book and say, "Thank you. Thank you. Thank you." Your voice is just waiting to move from the page to the shelves where the Universe takes care of the rest. Your job is to simply write. Mine is to guide you.

Chapter 3

Guidelines—An Overview

For all of us, it takes great courage and determination to walk consciously into the past, back into old pain to make sense of it—to open doors that have been locked, perhaps for decades—with an intention to let in the light, to give compassion to the younger person we were. This juncture calls for a willingness to embrace the past; let go of old anger, blame, and resentments; search our hearts for forgiveness for ourselves and for others; and move on.

Sometimes when life is difficult, you either become complacent or race quickly into what is next, not stopping to reflect on what occurred. This road, the one of writing your life stories, is the opposite of denial or giving up. It is one where often there is no road map. It is outside familiar territory; it pushes all comfort zones and boundaries and is definitely "the road less traveled." Yet paradoxically, it is also the one that leaves room for love and miracles to shine in.

And there is something mystical and magical about the writing process itself. We ask inside for guidance and become a conduit. Suddenly we no longer figure out what we want to say and how to say it. Our remembering comes from our listening, which becomes our writing on the page. We are taking dictation from what we hear. Each word flows naturally into a sentence, which breathes into the next and the next as a living entity. And it is these words, revealing new insights and memories, that become the catalyst for healing and understanding. It is here that tired or stuck energy gets lifted and a new lightness of being takes hold. New perceptions dance into consciousness accompanied by a sense of peace and often exhilaration. Our stories are being told. The truth is setting us free. We are writing ourselves home.

Writing Yourself Home

What does it mean to "write yourself home?" For me, it's an expression of writing that originates from deep in your heart and spirit. Your soul awaits you here. You only need to step to the side and let the words flow forth. There's a kindness here, a beckoning, a sense of wholeness. There's no need to edit from this place. Truth resonates here. Here you can go back to the difficult times of your past as well as the beautiful times with brand-new awareness and consciousness. It's about embracing the adult you are today as well as the life you lived before. Here you come home to yourself. The exercises in this book are designed to guide you through this process.

Writing yourself home gives you the opportunity to impart your truth. It may not be the exact way it happened. But it's your truth as to the way it happened, and that's vital. Each of us can occupy the same time and space with the same outer experience, yet it will be our inner experience and our personal perceptions that will determine its meaning.

Sometimes when memories surface that are painful, you may be tempted to write around them instead of through them. You might write in a fashion that sounds good in order to gain acceptance and approval—even from people who may be long since gone from your life—or even to try to look good to yourself. You might find yourself holding back or relating events in an apologetic or kind and poetic way that reads nicely but is not the truth, and you'll know it as you write it. It's important to lovingly and compassionately acknowledge that part of you that wants to hold back. Breathe and continue writing from a genuine place. Anything less would be cheating yourself and not worth the exercise.

May Sarton describes it this way, as quoted in *Writing from the Body* by John Lee (1994):

"I believe one has to stop holding back for fear of alienating some imaginary reader or real relative or friend and come out with personal truth. If we are to understand the human condition, and if we are to accept ourselves in all the complexity, self-doubt, extravagance of feeling guilt, joy, the slow freeing of the self to its full capacity for action and creation, both as human being and as artist, we have to know all we can about each other, and we have to be willing to go naked."

Going naked is a vulnerable place to be. As well, it is an authentic place to be. It gives you back your voice. It delves into shadows and rebirths the light. It portends forgiveness. It moves you along the path of resurrection that brings about closure to lifelong anger, regrets, resentments, and pain. Going naked allows you to call your spirit back. It doesn't happen all at once. It's a process that calls for patience, commitment, and faith.

No one—not me, your best friend, your partner, your mother—knows what you lived but you. Therefore, no one can go back and remember and heal these things for you. Other people may have been there, but their interpretations will be different from yours. When you acknowledge that which you have lived while staying open to a greater truth, the result will be a deeper clarity and compassion for you and for others.

Some years ago, while I wrote my life story, *On My Way Home: A Woman's Story*, it was as though an angel sat on my shoulder—which she probably was—and I too was an angel for myself. Instead of wallowing in my past, shaming myself, minimizing my life or embellishing it, I simply wrote from memory as it was given to me—each time asking for guidance and clarity, as I allowed my hands to move swiftly across the computer keyboard, neither editing nor judging, simply writing. It wasn't always easy. Sometimes I felt completely spent afterward and wondered what the point was of doing it. But I honoured my commitment to myself and the writing strengthened me. I didn't know this at the time. At the time I was just writing and willing to be as honest and as gentle with myself as I could be. I ask you to do the same.

You have the ability to heal the pain in your life. It is your perceptions of the things that occur, your interpretations of these events and your responses to them, that ultimately keep you in chains or set you free. Under everything that has happened to you, under all the pain, fear, chaos, and clutter is a much deeper meaning. And if you dare to look for the meaning, the gifts will reveal themselves.

Begin at the Beginning

Now that you have a better sense of why you are writing your stories, this section gives you an overview of what to expect along your memoir-writing journey.

For most writers, a blank page can be daunting. When looking at an empty page, panic can set in. "Where do I start? What do I say? How much should I say? How do I say it?" To help you deal with those kinds of questions and put your mind at ease, you need to prepare yourself in ways that can help you relax and look at each story as an honouring of yourself and as an exciting adventure. You begin with the first story—the one that calls to you. Perhaps it's an event you have been thinking about for a long time. That is the only one you need to think about for now.

Treat your pages as your dearest friend, one who is ready and willing to accept you as you are. Remember not to judge yourself or your writing when you put pen to paper (or fingers to keyboard). Judging yourself will slow you down or, worse, make you quit.

There are many themes or stories you may choose to write about, and you can write in whatever order calls to you. However, for the first story, I suggest you begin with "Gratitude". The reason for this is that your story of gratitude will be your touchstone—the story you can come back to when you're writing the ones that are difficult to tell. When you return to gratitude, you are right back in the present time and all that you have to be grateful for today. From this perspective, you see that the painful story that you will write about is in the past, and it can no longer hurt you unless you continue to focus on it; for whatever we focus on expands. Gratitude keeps us grounded in today; the more we focus on what we appreciate in our lives right here, right now, the happier we become.

For the stories of your life that are painful to recall, while writing and remembering, do not embody these memories. Instead, simply observe what happened from a safe distance as though you are watching it on a movie screen. You can also turn up the volume or turn it down. Make the picture larger or smaller. Brighter or dimmer. As a witness to what you see, you are also in the driver's seat, controlling all the gears.

This is an opportunity to be a loving and compassionate witness to a younger you—an earlier time when a situation arose that called for strength, courage and conviction to see you through.

In the beginning
There was a writing area, paper and pen and
Intention, courage, and commitment to "know thyself"

The Healing Power of Intention

Having a conscious intention towards something—whether it's about moving through our day with mindfulness, remembering to be patient when we are caught in traffic or whether it is to be kinder to ourselves and others when we're in the middle of a conflict—the act of having intention will bring about right mental and emotional alignment in order to achieve it. We are choosing to move through our world with consciousness—knowing that what we focus on grows. Our intention gives the Universe a signal that we are serious about what we want.

When you begin to write your memoir, choose to have the intention to let go of anything that is stopping you from having a happy life, free of resentments, anger, shame, and guilt. Have the intention to forgive the people in your life who have hurt you—

forgive them and yourself. Hold the intention to see the gifts and lessons in every story and especially hold the intention to love and honour your life. Honour yourself for the amazing human being and spirit you are. Honour yourself for the courage it takes to write your life stories with the conscious intention to heal any areas that are still hurting you. By doing this, you can live fully present in today with a song in your step and that no matter what the Universe may deliver, you have the tools, confidence, and resilience to move through it with ease and grace.

The Healing Power of Courage

It takes a great deal of courage to go back into old pain in order to release it and move forward. Yet it is necessary for your ultimate growth. You will find that the benefits outweigh the fear. Courage is often propelled by an honest commitment to heal your pain. Courage means that you feel the fear and do what it takes to move forward anyway. You take your pen and write into the hollow places that scare you and still continue to write until you are done. You uncover truths that have been buried deep inside you, perhaps for years, and the healing begins. You leap in an act of faith knowing in your heart that the net will be there. And it is. The Universe smiles at you and rewards you for your courage. Synchronicities—or "God-winks," as I like to call them—begin to happen. Things like when the telephone rings, and someone you have wanted to speak to for a long time is on the other end of the line, or when you cannot afford to go to a concert featuring your favourite band and a friend offers you a ticket that she cannot use, calling it an early birthday present.

Yes, courage has many unseen promises and rewards, especially the confidence to keep on keeping on. Writing your life stories with courage gives us inner confidence knowing the Universe has your back.

There is a lovely parable about a heron. A heron can stand in one spot seemingly for hours as though it is meditating. But in an unforeseen flash and with perfect precision, it will dart into the water, breaking the stillness with its beak and come up with a fish in its mouth. It is said that if the totem heron could speak, it would say, "Patience is not empty waiting. It is inner certainty."

That is the kind of faith I am asking of you as you re-write the painful stories of your life.

The Healing Power of Commitment

"Until one is committed, there is hesitancy, the chance to draw back, always ineffectiveness. Concerning all acts of initiative (and creation), there is one elementary truth—the ignorance of which kills countless ideas and splendid plans—the moment one definitely commits oneself, then providence moves too. All sorts of things occur to help one that would never otherwise have occurred. A whole stream of events, issues, and decisions, raising in one's favour all manner of unforeseen incidents and meetings and material assistance, which no one could have dreamed, would have come their way. Whatever you can do or dream, you can begin. Boldness has genius, power and magic in it. Begin it now."

– William Hutchison Murray

Self-Awareness Exercise

The following is an exercise in self-awareness to help you begin at the beginning. It is designed to tease out some internal answers and help you to excavate deeper truths about why you want to write your memoir. It will give you insights and clarity as you move forward.

 ### Time to Write

Four Questions: Regarding writing my memoir, what do I want, need, fear and hope for?

Write the following four questions down on a piece of paper ten times each. In other words, ask yourself the same question ten times and see what comes up for you. I have given examples. If they apply to you, please use them as your own. Be sure to write them, not type them. You want this to be a visceral experience. Pen to paper ensures that it will be.

Don't be concerned about repeating your answer. It simply means that this answer is particularly strong for you. The insights you will gain from doing this exercise may surprise you. They will reveal deeper truths about why you chose to undergo this memoir-writing journey and reinforce your commitment to it. You may think it's too easy and want to skip it. Or perhaps you think it's too hard and want to skip it. Do not. It is one of the most critical exercises in this book for teasing out your thoughts and feelings from your subconscious mind. Once you know what they are, you will feel way more inspired and empowered to begin. You will be reassured; this isn't just a passing fancy. You have opinions that matter about your life and what writing your memoir entails. You will become clear about what you want, what you need, what you fear, and what you hope for. This is you, sharing with yourself in the most intimate way, from the start. It only gets better from here.

Gather your journal, have a glass of water handy, and begin. Remember, have fun with it. You are a sleuth, a detective. Imagine being Sherlock Holmes or Nancy Drew and see what you discover inside the recesses of your own heart, mind, and soul.

Four Questions:
1. Regarding writing my life stories, what do I want?
2. Regarding writing my life stories, what do I need?
3. Regarding writing my life stories, what do I fear?
4. Regarding writing my memoir, what do I hope for?

The following are examples of ten answers to the question, "Regarding writing my life stories, what do I want?"

1. Regarding writing my life stories, what do I want?
   I want to have a living legacy for my children.
2. Regarding writing my life stories, what do I want?
   I want to reveal the truth.
3. Regarding writing my life stories, what do I want?
   I want to be free of the past and live more fully in today.
4. Regarding writing my life stories, what do I want?
   I want to understand myself better.
5. Regarding writing my life stories what do I want?
   I want to learn to forgive those who have hurt me, learn to forgive myself, and put closure on these past events and move on.
6. Regarding writing my life stories what do I want?
   I want to be grateful for my life and see the gifts that my stories have given me and how I am stronger for them.
7. Regarding writing my life stories what do I want?

I want to help inspire and empower others who may have had similar experiences.

8. Regarding writing my life stories what do I want?
   I want to embrace every experience in my life knowing that there has been a gift and lesson in each.

9. Regarding writing my life stories what do I want?
   I want to write my stories to essentially let go of them—that the process will free me from old wounds.

10. Regarding writing my life stories what do I want?
    I want to finally accept myself fully—all of me—remembering that I have always done the best I could at the time.

Once you have answered each of the four questions ten times this is what you do:

Sit with the answers to these questions and journal what they mean for you, what they brought up. Note any new awareness's, any ah-has, no matter how big or small they may seem.

Take your time. You have been excavating deep truths. My students have told me time and time again that when they answer these questions what at first didn't feel that profound was indeed a missing key that helped them move even further into their personal process of uncovering what has kept them stuck in their life for a long time.

I think this self-awareness exercise would make Socrates smile. "Know Thyself" is what he inscribed in the forecourt of the Temple of Apollo at Delphi. He said that to know thyself is the beginning of wisdom. He also said that people make themselves appear ridiculous when they try to know obscure things before they know themselves.

I agree, yet it is easier to study people, places, and things outside of ourselves than to the one we "should" know the most. Writing one's memoir or significant stories that have influence on our lives isn't for the faint of heart. In spite of that, you are here, and I am here as your friend, guide, and mentor, championing you all the way to the finish line. So is your Higher Self, by the way. You are not alone. As well, your angels are applauding you from heaven. Wave. See if you can do a "high five."

Chapter 4

Who Am I to Write my Life Stories?

Step 1

I don't have to ask you; I already know. You, like me and everyone else, have a mean-spirited critic in your head. In this chapter, I will show you how to stand up to that insensitive bully (often just a part of us who wants to protect us at all costs—it hasn't realized we are not two years old any longer and can fend for ourselves). Throughout this book, you will find lots of tools to stand up tall and strong to the part of you that would rather run, hide, or freeze. I also teach you compassionate ways to talk to that voice in your head that really and truly just believes it's doing its job.

As well, there are writing exercises, where you get to be the James Bond, Sherlock Holmes, or the detective of your choice, sleuthing into your own psyche to learn the you that was often hidden—even from yourself. As you write your memoir, you want to draw from your most authentic voice. The dominant/nondominant handwriting exercises with your inner child will reveal some of the deepest hidden messages that will empower you to do just that as you uncover and then integrate them into your adult self, the one who is writing this memoir.

Other People's Opinions

Are there people in your life whose opinions matter more than your own? And do you have what Oprah calls the "disease to please?" Would you rather stay obedient to someone else's ideas of what's good for you than rock the boat? Is that your usual modus operandi? Or are there other areas where you excel and don't worry about what people think? Often, it is the opinions of our family of origin (our parents and siblings) that trigger a reaction in us that makes us feel small and insignificant. Even if you rebel, at your core you fight against a subconscious belief of being unworthy. A belief you took on as a child that is still operating in the world, making an impact on how you navigate through your life.

I remember times when my life was going really well. My psychotherapy practice was doing great, I enjoyed my friendships, and felt safe and grounded—that is until I went back home to visit my family. Suddenly I was catapulted back to being eight years old again and whimpering around them. Or even if they didn't see that, I would take extra anti-anxiety medication to help myself get through it. And nothing even had to be said. It could just be a look and I'd interpret it as having done something wrong. And as strange as it may seem, for many of my clients—and perhaps it's true for you, too—some of those people who you have done headstands around are no longer even alive. Yet they have taken over even after their judgments stopped and they have been long gone from your life.

All of us want to live our lives with authenticity. Yet for many people who lost their voices long ago and who are afraid to speak their truth, it takes great courage to walk consciously into the past, back into old pain to make sense of it all. And even then, it takes additional courage to speak your truth out loud with conviction and authority.

Betty came to me with an amazing life story. She was in her late fifties and wanted to write it in the form of a memoir—that is until she told her sister, Suzy, about it. Her sister went berserk.

"How can you even consider writing that story and making it public? It will totally humiliate the entire family. What are you doing? Are you nuts?"

Growing up, Betty often felt that her voice and opinions didn't matter. Her sister's remarks took her aback even though she had done years of personal work on herself. She had also been my psychotherapy client, and by the time she realized she wanted to write her story, which had to do with alcoholism and the years it took her to recover, she was no longer blaming anyone in her family or any other circumstance for the choices she made. She was in a healthy place and only wanted to tell the story as it applied to herself and how she overcame years of addiction, what it cost her, and her recovery process. She wanted to write it to be an inspiration to other people from small towns with similar struggles. Her sister didn't want to hear any of that. It took a while working with Betty before she could value her own voice again and write her book in spite of what her sister said. She didn't write it "in spite." She wrote it in spite *of*, which is a different place. She was empowered, knew how far she had come, and realized that her sister's opinion did not need to silence her ever again. In the end, she decided not to publish her book but to offer it to her children so they could see her journey from the beginning, not just the places where she messed up, which she feared were the only ones they would remember. Writing that book and sharing it with her kids was a huge personal catharsis, as well as the beginning of healing for her and her children.

In the self-reflection questionnaire you answered in the last chapter, what stood out the most for you with respect to what you want, what you need, what you fear and what you hope for?

Now is the time, more than ever, to protect your boundaries and give yourself permission to live the life you have dreamed of living. Call your power back and choose to walk as though you are unstoppable. I'm walking briskly right beside you.

Choice Point: Should I Kill Him or Kiss Him?

In the late eighties, I was seeing a shrink, Dr. Sherman, on a steady basis as I was in and out of psych wards. However, at the same time, I did everything I could to improve my life—including going back to school to become a psychotherapist.

One day I picked up a book by Natalie Goldberg. I recognized that her style and mine were practically the same, only she had named her process. To me, it was just natural, but I also knew that if I followed her system, I too could be a writing coach like she was. It was the most excited I had been in years and could hardly contain my enthusiasm when I saw Dr. Sherman next and told him what I had discovered.

Dr. Sherman seemed to be a psychiatrist of a different breed, at least in my opinion. I could sense he truly cared about me. I often read him things I wrote in my diary because it was easier back then to write them than to express them out loud without having written prompts. He encouraged me, and I'd leave his office each time feeling lighter, that I did have a chance, that I could learn how to improve my life. He gave me more confidence than anyone else at that time so you can imagine my excitement when I got to his office to tell him my news.

"Doc," I declared with unusual optimism, "I read this book over the weekend by this woman who writes books on writing. She is also a writing coach and I think I can do what she does. I think I can also facilitate writing groups—teach people what comes naturally to me."

I waited for, "June [I was June back then, not Junie]. That's fantastic. I'm thrilled for you." Instead he looked up at me, which in itself was rare—as he had a habit of drawing mandalas while I sat in the chair in front of his desk. Still, he listened better than any shrink I had seen in prior years and, in fact, better than anyone else I knew.

He looked up, and I think I saw his eyes for the first time as he stared directly into mine and said, "Do you have a degree in English or English literature?"

"No," I said.

"Have you ever done anything like this before?"

"No," I whispered.

"Don't you think it would take a lot of chutzpah?" he continued.

Yes froze in my throat so I remained mute.

Suddenly, without warning a huge smile broke out on his face as he declared, "June, my dear, I say go for it."

I'm sure I choked and sputtered as I finally stopped holding my breath and exhaled for the first time in minutes.

By now he was laughing. "Gotcha, didn't I?" I wanted to kill him and kiss him at the same time. So, I did go for it, and the rest is history. The same year I hung my shingle as a psychotherapist was the year I offered writing groups. It was the early nineties.

Why am I telling you this story? Because I know that even when you recognize an inspired idea, something that comes to you from a place deep within you, if you don't have the confidence to stand up for your truth, someone else's opinion could knock it over in a tender heartbeat.

If that doctor had been seriously interrogating me about my credentials and the chutzpah it would take to do what I proposed, I never would have chosen this sacred path, which has definitely been my dharma. I simply wasn't able to stand on my own feet with confidence and would have let his opinion matter more than my own. After all, he was a doctor. A psychiatrist who knew my history. In my mind, back then, I didn't stand a chance.

Even though you have a place within you that knows that writing your memoir is a soul's calling, you need to stand tall in that knowledge so that no one's opinion about it can change your mind.

"One can never consent to creep
when one feels an impulse to soar."
– Helen Keller

I know you have an impulse to soar and no one else can do it for you.

No matter who scolded you when you were young, no matter whether or not you were abused, neglected, abandoned, scorned, or bullied, you have the ability right now to take control back into your life.

And if you are going to write your memoir, and be free from the residue of the past—which could be anger, rage, resentment, worry, guilt, shame, insecurity et cetera—then it's best that you use the power of the pen to help you move through it and the tools laid out in this chapter and the rest of the book will get you there. You do not want to stay in resentment.

If your goal is to write your memoir to cast blame, you will never be free. If your goal is to heal whatever is left unhealed and move forward, then you have before you the most excellent opportunity to turn your life into a beautiful living legend. If more of your life was painful experiences than happy ones, declare out loud, "The buck stops here." You can change it for yourself and others by making yours a spectacular life.

The Angry, Blaming, Uncensored Letter

One of the most effective antidotes for painful emotions you feel but keep inside of you or express in ways that do not serve you is writing an angry blaming letter. It is 100 percent safe as long as you don't put it in an email and press send. It's not only effective in its ability to dissipate any anger, blame, and resentment you may be still carrying, it is also incredibly satisfying in the moment.

The idea is to write a blaming, angry, uncensored letter—again, that you never send—as a way of releasing what has been stored up inside of you. It is a safe and healthy way of getting your rage out of your body and onto the page, which won't get angry back.

If the person you are angry with is still in your life today, by the time you're ready to deal directly with him or her, you will be much calmer and more centred. It is also possible that you will have a deeper understanding of what's underneath the anger. Often, it is fear or sadness. And, if you continue to stay with the process, you will most likely discover that it has nothing to do with the person with whom you feel angry. It's usually from a much earlier time in your life, and this person triggered your unhealed wounds.

Until you heal them, it's likely that you will project your anger, hurt, pain, fear, et cetera, onto people in your life, causing untold hurt and drama that I'm certain you would rather not have. This is one of the many healing exercises that will help you write your memoir from a place of healing, grounding discernment and growth.

Your Inner Child

Within you is an inner child who wants to dance and fly free. She doesn't want to be burdened with rules, especially other people's. And she wants and needs to trust you—the adult you—to take care of her. No one better than you knows what you have lived and therefore no one better than you has the ability to go back and heal those parts of you that still hurt. This is a stellar opportunity to reparent the child who walks inside your adult's body still afraid to show up fully in life.

Loving yourself is the greatest gift you can give to yourself and everyone else you encounter throughout your day. When you fill our own well, you feel satisfied, happy, and nourished and then when there are requests from others, you have the energy to come to them from a full open heart. You can say yes or no without attachment, resentment, or fear. Even if your reply to someone's request is no, it's because you chose what is best in honouring yourself. By practicing self-love you can express your decision with kindness instead of being defensive or, worse, passive aggressive—smiling all the while resenting the task you do for someone when you simply don't want to be doing it. It is so much easier to say, in a kind way, "I know you need the help right now, and honestly, I would love to be able to give it to you. However, I need to say no as I am replenishing my energy in order to stay healthy."

Notice what comes up inside of you when reading this last sentence. If you are okay with it, you are in a good place to implement healthy boundaries and not say yes, when you mean no. People who love and respect you will honour your decision.

If, however, you got sweaty palms or noticed your heart beating faster or found yourself thinking about someone in particular and their reaction to you and it made you feel sick inside, then you have some work to do. There's no judgment. All of this is sleuth work, remember. Just an opportunity to come to your life in a way that will serve you, so that you can write your life stories—no matter who may think otherwise.

Picture yourself walking into a room and you noticing a young child curled up in the corner, crying. Imagine you walking over to that child with deep concern and compassion and asking her or him what is wrong. Between sobs he tells you that his father got mad and yelled at him because he didn't finish his homework. He goes on to explain it was because he was so tired. He hasn't slept in many days because of the arguments at home. He is afraid.

Would you say to that child, "Well it serves you right. You should have done your homework. How do you expect to succeed in life if you fail school?"

Of course you wouldn't say that. Isn't it more likely you would kneel down to comfort the child, tell him you are so sorry that his father yelled at him and that there is fighting at home and he feels afraid. Wouldn't you hold him and dry his tears and show him you care?

When you are treated badly, is there a part of you that believes that you deserve it? That you are not worthy of kindness and love? Do you take on the verbal admonitions of others long after they have said them and beat yourself up for a long, long time with the words that were said to you when you were a child or teenager? As I stated earlier, if you have taken over where people who punished you years ago left off, even if they are no longer alive, their words still reverberate in your head and cause deep grief inside your psyche.

We say things to ourselves we would never say to anyone else and what's worse, over time, we start to believe them and believe that is who we are.

The Seven-Year Old Bus Driver

The words you say to yourself and the thoughts you think about yourself have enormous power. over your life. If you have been thinking them long enough, they become your beliefs. And it's your beliefs that drive the bus—beliefs you often took on before the age of seven. Know that whatever you focus on expands, making it more and more difficult to move out of that groove that causes the needle to stay stuck, deepening the groove while the words and behaviours repeat over and over again.

Today is a brand-new day to become curious about nurturance versus self-harm. Are the words you speak about yourself and others kind or unkind? Does the food you eat support your body? Are your relationships healthy and empowering?

The most important thing is to learn to love yourself in ways that perhaps you never have. Today you have the opportunity to nurture yourself above anyone else knowing it is paramount for feeling good and anything else is simply non-negotiable.

Your honest investment in nurturing yourself and practising radical self-care and self-love will empower you to write the most magnificent memoir of all. You will write it from a feel-good awesome state as you relate the events from your past. You will even be able to make the leap—that inside these same events that hurt you are gifts ready to be unwrapped.

Are you willing to up the ante, congratulate, and celebrate yourself for your courage and tenacity to overcome hurdles for your ability to stand up again and again no matter how many times you may have fallen? No matter how weary you have been or how hopeless it may have felt. The fact you are here ready to write your memoir means you have already won. You have survived all that has befallen you in the past. Now, it's beyond survival. It's about falling in love with your own heart—your loving, sensitive, kind nature and your tenacity and ability and willingness to move beyond your comfort zone in order to learn and accomplish new things.

I will help reinforce these fabulous qualities. Let me teach you to navigate your life in the best way possible, no matter how many times your heart has been broken and in a world that often seems crazy and out of control.

The following is an opportunity to love the child that still lives inside of you. To give her or him all the love and compassion you can muster. After all, who knows better than you what that younger you experienced? Again, who better than you to give yourself what you need?

You will access and embrace the precious, innocent little girl or boy who was once you. The one that went unnoticed, became shy or invisible or, conversely, rebelled in order to be seen or heard. This is your inner child who still resides within you, and as you can imagine, if his or her voice was squelched, the unhealed wounds of this child are still present in your unconscious today and most likely running the show and driving that bus.

It may have been so long ago when you first felt no one was listening or cared about your opinions—or perhaps even loved you— that you don't remember how it started. But remembering the exact time or incident isn't as important as knowing what happens inside of you in present-day, how you feel when you feel neglected, invisible, unacknowledged, or unvalued.

Perhaps you are timid and shy and rarely speak, just in case you are criticized, especially if you are hoping to impress a person!

At the other end of the spectrum, that inner child may be rebelling, defending her story until someone will listen, and when they don't, you become hurt, frustrated, and angry and may be keeping score, ready to retaliate.

Right off the bat, please know this is not your fault. It's likely you never had a role model to help guide you in communicating your feelings in a grounded, rational way. Under your shyness or, conversely, your anger, is the you who is heartbroken, desperate for someone to understand you, believe in you. Listen to you. See you. Take the time to know you.

Events in our lives remind us of past experiences. Everything outside of us is a reflection of our inner lens, the eyes we see it with. When you have been hurt in the past, the things you see, hear, taste, touch, or smell can become triggers that will cause you to react, even when your reaction has nothing to do with the present situation. When you heal the trigger, the event becomes neutral. You no longer react. You stay present in today. For instance, a loud bang is no longer a bomb that exploded when you were a soldier. It's a car backfiring on the street. You do not need to be afraid.

Think about an incident in your life when you felt ignored, rejected, or dismissed and that your feelings just didn't matter. Choose the first person that comes to mind.

What is happening? What is being said or not said? How are you responding? Are you heartbroken?

Do you feel numb? Do you feel like you've lost the battle? Do you feel that there's no point in saying anything, that nothing ever changes? You don't want to rock the boat in case it gets worse? Or do you get angry and retaliate with your words or actions?

What if that same person you felt was not listening to you, even ignoring you or giving you a look of dismissal or disdain, sat down beside you, looked directly into your eyes and said, "I am here now. Please, share with me what's going on. I am listening. I want to be your friend and I want to understand. I know I haven't been good at that in the past but I want to make an effort now, please let me in. I'm sorry I have hurt you so."

Notice how you feel in your body. Does your heart expand when you hear this? Conversely, does it make you angry because it didn't happen this way and probably never would?

Underneath all of that, wouldn't you give anything to know that this person cares for you this way—that you do matter to him or her? That you are enough, that you are seen as worthy?

Well, you can't change the how the past unfolded for you. Nor can you make someone say those things. But what if you said them to you? To the parts of you that ache to have them said by another? After all you are the only person who knows the extent of your disappointments, heartbreaks and regrets. Therefore, no one more than you knows the words you need to hear to fill your heart with tenderness and open to love again. Each part of you that has closed down needs more love not less in order to blossom and come alive once again.

Reparenting Your Inner Child

This next exercise asks you to reparent your inner child, giving him or her the unconditional love he or she deserves. You are being asked to love yourself the way no one has ever loved you before.

In order to do that, you need to get to know your child-self. To help you to do this, once again, go back and review your answers to the four questions: what you want, need, fear, and hope for in order to write your memoir and ultimately have a more fulfilled life.

Once you have reviewed this, it's time to have a dialogue with your inner child—get to know some of the reasons that have been holding her or him back.

Time to Write a Letter to Your Inner Child

You will need paper or a journal and pens, crayons, or coloured markers.

Use a pen to represent your nurturing adult self, the one who is your present age today, with your dominant hand.

Use a crayon or coloured marker with your nondominant hand to represent your child-self.

Begin by picking up your pen with your dominant hand and write the following:

"My dearest _____ (write your name that you were called as a child). I know you have been hurting for a long time. And I know I haven't taken the time to listen to you. I am truly sorry. But I am here now. I want to be your friend. I want you to feel safe with me, and I know it will take a bit of time to trust me. I'm sorry it took me so long to show up and tell you this. Darling, what do you need to help you feel safe?"

Now, with your nondominant hand, let your child-self choose a coloured crayon or marker print what he or she wants. If you are not used to writing with your nondominant hand, it will feel awkward. Let it. Don't try to make it neat and tidy. If it takes a whole page to write or scribble a few words, that's okay. Let your child-self say as much or as little as he or she needs to.

After every comment, no matter what that hurt part of yourself blurts out, always respond with compassion and love.

You can ask your child how old she is and where she is. She might say, "I'm under the bed and I'm never coming out," like mine did. She might say, "I'm sitting in a classroom waiting for Mommy to come and get me. She's late. Only the janitor is here." She might say, "I'm sitting in my room playing with my toys." You can ask who else is with her.

Keep the conversation going.

Your child self may recite a time where you were punished or abused in some way. You can now stand up for her or him by writing a letter to that person.

Tell your child that you are so sorry there was no one there to protect her, but you are going to be her voice now.

This is your opportunity to reclaim your voice. Perhaps it's a voice you have kept hidden all your life. You have every right to feel furious. Get your anger onto the page. The same goes for frustration, numbness, or the shame you've carried all these years from someone's ignorant comments or behaviour. Write wherever you are right now.

Numb? You can start with, "I don't even feel it anymore. You did such a good job at making me feel ashamed, I lost my confidence about most things. But not anymore."

Keep going as you imagine how that child or teenager in you must have felt and give her back her voice.

Feel compassion for the you that endured that pain and say everything you would have wanted to say then.

You write into your authentic voice until it comes tearing out from under the barricades into the fresh air, still tentative perhaps, but stay with it.

On the page, you are now reaching beyond the surface words, the hiding, the pretending, and you say it all. Into the privacy of your journal, there is no need to hold back. Write fear-ward. It's your key to authenticity—to freedom. It's okay. You are safe. Just write until you have said everything. Afterward, go out and do something nurturing and fun. Ask the child in you what he or she wants and then do it. Maybe it's to play on the beach, get a massage, take a day trip somewhere where you've been wanting to go. Maybe it's a dinner out with a good friend. Maybe it's a trip to the dollar store to get coloured stickers to put in your journal that say things like "Well done" and "You rock!"

Here's an example of a dialogue I had with my inner child many years ago:

Me (as an adult): How are you, sweet little Junie?

Child-Self: [she picks up a black crayon and scribbles] Why would you care?

Me: Thank you for telling me that. Of course I care.

Child-Self: You do not, and I hate you.

Me: I am so sorry I have hurt you this much. How old are you, sweetheart?

Child-Self: I'm seven.

Me: Where are you?

Child-Self: I'm under the bed.

Me: Why are you there? Are you frightened?

Child-Self: [grabs black crayon and in capital letters writes] I'M NEVER COMING OUT.

Me: Do you want to talk about it, honey?

Child: NO. You never listen.

As we continued our dialogue, I learned that the child in me desperately wanted me to leave the man I lived with, that he was controlling, that I let him take over our lives, and that she never had a voice.

I promised I would listen and would love her more and would commit to her more than ever. I did my best to keep that promise. It didn't happen right away. I guess I needed some more sledgehammers first. But then I renewed my promise and would show up every day on the page and invite her in. I let her speak her truth. I gave her back her voice—my voice, of vulnerability and fear that I hid from because I didn't want to face the fact that she was right. I so wanted the relationship to work out. But he was a bully, and just as I never stood up to a family member as a child and for many years as an adult, I couldn't stand up to him either.

My dialogue with that vulnerable part of me showed me in living colour what it cost me to stay in an abusive relationship. Eventually, I got the courage to leave. I gave myself the gift of loving the parts of me that I buried for so long. I stopped abandoning myself. It all started in my journal with loving, acknowledging, and listening deeply to the voice that I knew was telling the truth all along. That of my inner child. The wise, scared and most honest part of me.

Here's another example of something I wrote to help that child in me heal the pain I felt when I was only eleven years old.

My grade six teacher was mean and shamed me almost daily. This writing example came after giving myself time to integrate what happened—after allowing my child-self, who was traumatized, to scream out her hurt and rage onto the page. Once she felt vindicated, having been witnessed and protected by me, I, the adult, was able to write another letter from a centred, grounded place in me.

I imagined my teacher listened to me with an open heart. A few days later, I was ready to write another letter. This time it was from her to me. I imagined how she would have responded after listening with compassion, truly hearing me. She wrote me a letter of apology. The wounded child in me couldn't hear those words often enough. There was one more letter—it was one where I was able to fully forgive her.

Here are my letters:

"Miss Simmons, how could you? How could you! How could you have ever been a teacher, a teacher to little kids? Did you have any idea what you did to us? Did to me. I hated you for it.

Okay, I've gone beyond it now, but does it make it right? No, I will never condone your horrible, despicable behaviour. Teachers are supposed to model kindness and compassion, hone confidence in the students they teach. Help them with the tough subjects, foster curiosity, and make learning fun. Not you. You bully. You despicable bully. I was only eleven years old. Eleven for God's sake!

Did you have any idea what was happening to me at home? Did you have any idea that school was going to be my escape? School was not just a prison; it was a torture chamber. You hated me, and you made it known every single day. You shamed me again and again in front of my classmates. When my marks were the lowest, you called them out as an example for the other kids of what not to do. You were hideous. Demanding that Steve and I stay after school, hovering over us and telling us that we were stupid, that we were a disgrace and you would fail us. And you did. You did fail us! I went home on the last day of school with great big red FAILED scribbled across my report card. Oh, I can imagine your smug satisfaction when you did that.

You have no idea how you ruined my life for so many years. How timid, insecure, and shy I became. How I wore a million masks to hide the shame that I felt for being stupid. I was afraid of everyone and everything. The only thing that saved me was my little red diary with its lock and key. I poured my aching heart onto the pages. But

I was also terrified my mother would find it. Or my brother. And Marshal did find it, and the night he locked me in the bathroom, turned out the light so it was pitch black, and I was already scared to death, he started reading it out loud on the other side of the door and taunting me. I can't remember how long it took me to ever write again. I did, but I burned the pages right afterward.

Miss Simmons, you had an opportunity to make life a little easier for me. With kindness. With patience and love. With something that would make me not want to run away forever, or at least find a way to still the relentless voices in my head that kept telling me to just kill myself and get it over with.

It has been over half a century since I was shamed by you. Since I felt sickened every morning when I woke up and had to trudge to school, across the creek to Baycrest Avenue Public School. Lots of days I simply stayed at the creek watching the baby frogs leaping up on the banks and the tadpoles swimming without a care in the world. Oh, I knew I would pay big time for playing hooky, but I couldn't help it. Facing you was so much worse.

Now over fifty years later, what do you have to say to me?"

"Dear June,

Words can't make it better. But if they could, I would tell you how truly sorry I am. If I could do it over, I would take you into my heart and offer you love and compassion. Of course I saw your pain. Of course I saw how frightened you were. And it pleased me to lash out at you, and I am so ashamed. I had my own struggles and unresolved pain, and it was my way to take it out on the beautiful children who came to me to educate them, encourage them, and teach in a way that they would succeed. But this isn't about me. It's about you, dearest June. I remember you, and I remember how horrible I was to you, and I am so very, sorry. Thank you for coming to me so many years later to call me on what I did to you. I can't take it back. I am only grateful that you moved on. That somehow along life's path you were able to move beyond the horrors of your young life and make a good life for yourself.

Dear Miss Simmons, I am sorry too for whatever happened to you in your life that made you be that way. I hope you have since forgiven yourself and have found peace in your heart. I forgive you."

The name of this chapter is "Who Am I to Write My Life Stories?" I hope that by now, you are much closer to knowing exactly who you are to write your memoir. As you work through the exercises with your detective hat on, you must wear your special spectacles—a prerequisite for the job. They have a "C" symbol on the frame, which stands for compassion, their own unique brand. It is only through these lenses—the lenses of the child—that you will learn of her or his innocence and why she or he may still be afraid to come out fully in the world. Each exercise has been carefully designed for you to claim back your voice and your life. To fill your own awesome shoes as an adult, to move forward with self-assurance as well as tender appreciation for all that you have lived. "It is in our vulnerability where our strengths lies"—A Course In Miracles. In the next chapter, you will anchor in these new concepts and powerful tools even deeper as you proceed in writing your life stories.

Chapter 5

Looking Inward with Eyes of Love

Step 2

I n this chapter, Step 2 is an invitation to go beyond what is probably comfortable to you, in order to take stock of how awesome you are. That's right. You are probably someone who has had other people's lives mean more than your own, and now I ask you to turn the tables on that so that you can write your memoir from a place of true self-appreciation, self-respect, and self-love that comes from an honest look at who you are at your core. Your strengths, your fears, your vulnerabilities, your humanness, your awesomeness. All of it, valuing it all.

I want you to stay open and positive with the inquisitiveness of a child, to look at your life and all you have achieved in both your inner and outer expressions of yourself that has made you into the person you are today.

It is from this perspective, one of valuing yourself more than anyone else ever could that will bring out the voice that will write your treasured stories and celebrate your life's journey.

You transfer that energetic celebration to your future readers as they ingest each of your stories that go from your heart to theirs—just as you hope it will.

Just as these words that flow out of my fingertips onto this screen—which is an intention set forth to transmit my love to you—I have confidence you will receive it in kind. I have come to know that this is how our benevolent Universe works. The energy we send out is received in kind, even if we can't see it. Believing it first is the key. Most of us have been taught that seeing is believing. Actually, it's the other way around. You must believe it first, and then you will see it. Believe you will write the most awesome stories reflecting the experiences of your life. Of course you will. By knowing this truth in your heart, what will come out of your fingertips onto the pages will reflect exactly that. I know this. You are about to know it too. And that is music to my ears, heart, and soul.

You learned in Chapter 3 the importance of setting an intention; let this intention be set with a prayer. Read it out loud to yourself and ingest the words, the meaning, the intention, and the love in which you desire to bring it from your lips to God's ears.

Dear God,

Please guide me out of the shadows and into the Light. Help me to take the words I use against myself and transform them into words and acts of loving kindness. Help me when I am stuck and when I'd rather stay that way than face the challenge of moving forward.

Teach me to know the truth about myself ... the places where I hide my beauty from the world and even from myself. Show me how to break free of this self-defeating trap. Teach me to accept and nurture the parts of me that are still learning, still growing up and making mistakes. Teach me to accept that I will always be learning, growing up, and making mistakes and, therefore, to be kinder to myself in all situations. Help me to recognize what my true gifts are. Give me the courage and strength to believe in them. To believe in me. To reach for them one small step at a time. Teach me to slow down. To breathe. To relax. To know I am safe. And to explore the world as the small child, with innocence, curiosity, and enthusiasm.

And finally, let me express myself wholly from my integrated heart and mind so that I can walk in this world with the qualities of joy, strength, passion, appreciation and gentleness. Add to that honesty, gratitude, and kindness to myself and to others. Help me write my memoir from my Highest Self so that it will be for the highest good of all concerned. And thank you, dear God for all your many blessings.

Amen.

With this prayer, you have set an intention to see all the things you have done right in your life. Even when you made choices that were not aligned with your highest good, your true nature, they came from the consciousness of who you were then. If you could have done it differently you would have. You were doing the best you knew how to at the time. Today you would make a different choice, given the same circumstances. Am I correct? Of course, because you have learned. That's how we grow—through choices that don't serve us in order to make choices that do.

Have some of the choices you made in the past left you feeling guilty and with regrets? Do you wish you had done it differently? Was there a time that something you said or did cause a rift between you and someone else that was the catalyst for a friend to leave and never return? Perhaps it was a lover or even your spouse. Perhaps it was a choice that cost you your job. We cannot go back and change what we said or did, but we can think back about it with compassion for the parts of us that are still hurting. As well, a sincere apology, no matter how much time has passed, is always welcomed. It is never too late to say, "I'm sorry."

And, as we move forwards with newfound awareness, we can do it with eyes wide open and make solid sound choices leading to decisions we're proud of. The following poem, "An Autobiography in 5 Chapters," from The Tibetan Book of Living and Dying by Sogyale Rinpche, indicates the patterns that most of us go through while learning how to navigate life in sound and healthy ways.

"Chapter 1
I walk down the street. There is a deep hole in the sidewalk. I fall
in. I am lost… I am hopeless. It isn't my fault. It takes forever to
find a way out.

Chapter 2
I walk down the same street. There is a deep hole in the sidewalk. I
pretend I don't see it. I fall in again. I can't believe I'm in the same
place. But it isn't my fault. It still takes a long time to get out.

Chapter 3
There is a deep hole in the sidewalk. I see it is there. I still fall in. It's a habit. My eyes are open. I know where I am. It is my fault. I get out immediately.

Chapter 4
I walk down the same street. There is a deep hole in the sidewalk. I walk around it.

Chapter 5
I walk down another street."

This poem teaches how to walk down another street. Step 2 may be one of the most challenging steps of all because sometimes people who have approached life in service to others have a difficult time knowing how to look after themselves well, to praise themselves and move from feelings of worthlessness to feelings of worthiness— worthwhile and worthy of all the riches in the kingdom because it's their birthright. And it's yours and it's mine.

Are you someone who, when someone says you look beautiful or they admire something you have achieved, deflects it or says, "Oh, it's nothing."

It is paramount that you learn to receive in equal amounts to what you give, as it is the same energy and the same art in motion. And in doing so, you open to the Abundant Nature of the Universe to flow through you and to you.

What does this have to do with writing your memoir, you might ask? It's addressing the question in Chapter 4, "Who am I to write a memoir?" If you do not fully value who you are, it's unlikely that you will move ahead and write your memoir. You simply do not think anyone would read it, or they might criticize you if you did write it, and if their opinion matters more than your own, it becomes a vicious circle.

As stated earlier, your beliefs run the show and often drive the bus and have more power than the temporary part of you that says, "I can do it." The truth is, you can do it, but first you have to be honest and know that if there are parts of you that doubt you have what it takes to write this book, haven't you stopped yourself long enough? Now it is time to summon up the courage to move out of your comfort zone of negativity. Every time you notice that you are putting yourself down, change that thought immediately. Awareness is key. Apologize to the innocent child within you who you have promised to honour and cherish. It may take a while to get into the habit of this, but the more you do it, the easier it gets. Begin to acknowledge every compliment that comes your way. Take it in and then offer a sincere thankyou in return.

Of course, a million people can tell you something awesome about yourself but if at the core you don't believe it, it runs off like water off a duck's back. Why? Remember, you are writing a memoir from the place where you stand tall, honouring all that you have lived, learned, and loved. From this place and by gathering the choices you have made, you can look back with twenty-twenty vision (which is nearly impossible while life is happening 'to" us, up close and personal) and, with maturity and newly found wisdom, take ownership for those choices. It is from this place you will receive the greatest understanding and insight and make the most impact on those who read your stories. Most of us want to leave behind that which life has taught us—so that what we have learned can serve others. Yet it is our light that frightens us the most as is told so eloquently in Marianne Williamson's passage in her 1989 spiritual best-seller, A Return to Love.

"Our deepest fear is not that we are weak. Our deepest fear is that we are powerful beyond measure. It is our light, not our darkness that most frightens us. We ask ourselves, who am I to be brilliant, gorgeous, talented, fabulous? Actually, who are you not to be? You are a child of God. Your playing small does not serve the world. As we are liberated from our own fear, our presence automatically liberates others."

Last year I worked with a beautiful man, Brandon, who wanted to write a book about someone else's life as a tribute to him and his family. He talked at length about how he admired this particular person who had since died. He outlined this man's strengths and how much he accomplished, considering he lived his life from a wheelchair. I knew from the beginning that Brandon identified with the man he admired but he was too shy and unassuming to recognize it. He didn't see his own life being important enough to write about. I took it slowly and cautiously until I knew he was ready to see this for himself.

At that point, I said, "Brandon, do you realize what you admire in F.L. is all the qualities that you have within yourself? And do you see that your life and your history has followed a parallel path?" Well, he did see it. And he was blown away. Up until that point, what became blatantly obvious to Brandon had been invisible. He was now ready to write his own story. As we worked together, he was able to release the guilt and shame he had for choices he made, realizing they were not his fault. He could now reach in and pull out the beautiful choices he made as well, the ones that brought joy to himself and others, for his personal and professional achievements and mostly for his beautiful, kind, and loving heart. He remembered some of the loving things that had been said to him over his lifetime and wasn't deflecting them. He could now see, appreciate, and be thankful that he was, in fact, deserving of such praise. Each time he came to a session it seemed his smile grew wider, his stride was stronger, and he stood taller (which was lot for a man already six feet, four inches in height).

Where might you be holding back? Here is your new mantra:

> *"Oh mirror—when I look at you*
> *I can see my reflection oh so true*
> *I see the love within my eyes*
> *That sparkle and twinkle, that are so wise*
> *I smile at myself and give me a wink*
> *Oh to think I wasn't good enough*
> *Or that I didn't really matter.*
> *It's not the truth, I am enough.*
> *I do matter.*
> *I am beautiful.*
> *I am oh so beautiful. "*

Self-Reflection and Taking Stock with Ease and Joy.

With this brand-new attitude, I have a journal writing exercise for you.

Journal Writing Exercise: Your Legacy
Use coloured markers to have a more vivid sensory experience.

Give yourself at least one hour of uninterrupted time for the following exercise. Grab your journal, a pen, and a glass of water. I always like to have a candle lit as well and even have crystals and other precious objects that have meaning for me as I write. You may like to do the same.

In your journal, you are going to take stock of all the things you have done in your life that you are proud of. What legacy do you want to leave your kids, if you have kids? And if you don't—what legacy do you want to leave yourself and to those who have known you, whose lives you have touched in myriad ways, probably without knowing how much. How can you measure the little seeds that are planted by a word, a look, a kind gesture, that transform a person's life? A legacy is not just what you have done, it's who you are!

This is your story and the intention to give it is that of celebrating and honouring yourself. This is the time to pull out all the stops. Every time you were told don't talk about yourself, you'll get a swelled head—it's okay. Break all the rules and take an inventory of your inner and outer world. The things you did and the choices you made that, in retrospect, you feel good about. These are the times you found a healthier way of moving beyond situations that were challenging or where you had to even physically remove yourself because it was dangerous to be there or the times when you made a choice that didn't have the best outcome but, looking back from today's C specs "Compassionate Spectacles" you can see how it led to something else that became a learning experience and therefore a gift.

What insecurities did you have to overcome in order to achieve certain successes? What courses or schools did you have to attend in order to pass exams that led to a step up the ladder in your chosen field?

What things did you do or what thoughts or prayers did you offer when no one was watching and that no one would even know about in order to better someone else's life?

What do others come to you asking advice about?

What about your creative self? What do you love to do in your spare time that makes your heart sing? In fact, do you like to sing? Dance? Garden? Do you love to take pictures—do you take yourself on hikes, explore nature, travel? How often do you do the things you love? Is there room for growth here? Not only do the answers to these questions for the purpose of this exercise enlighten you, they may also be the things you begin to seek out for future days and years ahead. Let the inspiration of that be your prime motivator.

This is not a time for judgment. It is a time for reflection, observation, discernment, inspiration and hope.

What would your best friends say they value the most in you?

Who are your role models? What is it about that person or people that you like, love, respect, and admire?

Did you know you can't see in someone or something that which is not in you first? It is impossible. I'll prove it to you and at the end of this little experiment, you will have affirmations that you don't have to grow into. They will be the real deal right now that you will not be able to refute. This is one of my favourite exercises to offer my clients. I am so excited to be offering it to you.

Wherever you are right now, stop reading and look up and notice your surroundings. Choose one thing in your environment that you like. It could be a vase, a painting—It could be flowers, or it could be the ring you are wearing on your finger.

Next, I want you to write three adjectives about that object that you like and write them in a list down the page.

Say it's a painting of the ocean. What three words would you use to describe what you like about it?

The ocean:

1. Expansive
2. Always in motion
3. Blue = peaceful, calm

Now in front of the three words you chose, write the words, "I am."

It will look like this:

1. Expansive: I am expansive
2. Always in motion: I am always in motion
3. Blue: I am peaceful and calm

Again, we can never see outside of us that which is not inside of us first. Knowing this, it's easier to understand how your outer world is a reflection of your inner one.

Now, do this exercise again about the people in your life whom you admire.

Do you admire them because of their courage, their ability to take risks, their sense of humour? You couldn't enjoy these features in them if they weren't already something you have within you that resonates deeply with who you are and that you appreciate. Take this in. For these are your qualities too.

Continue to write about all the things in your life that have worked in the past or are working for you now. Instead of thinking about what went wrong and what's wrong with you and your life—

turn that on its head and think about everything that is right, from the new perspective you are cultivating.

That's your job from this day until your last day, and since you won't know when that will be, it's your new modus operandi to take notice of all that you have and have become so that more will be drawn to you.

Keep a journal just for gratitude and write down all the things that you are grateful for. Include your bed and the faucet that you can simply bring a glass to, turn the nob and nourish your body with refreshing water where many cannot. No longer take luxuries for granted.

Gratitude is an attitude. It is an attitude that no matter what is going on in your life, you are able to recognize the good—that which is working—the events and moments that warm you, bring you joy, and help you see and acknowledge those things that lift your spirits. They are everywhere if you just let yourself be open to them. Have you ever walked down the street on a day you felt particularly sad or lonely and a stranger smiled at you and in an instant, your heart opened? Even such a seemingly small gesture can give meaning to your day. Did you know that the fastest way to raise your vibration is to smile?

Gratitude is also the first spiritual law of abundance. As we appreciate and are grateful for where we are and what we have right now, we create the conditions for abundance to show up. Living in gratitude raises our vibration and we become an open conduit for God's grace to enter.

Annie Lavack, a New-Thought minister, put it this way, in her story, *Blessings Along the Way* taken from my book, *Re-Write Your*

Life: A Transformational Guide to Writing and *Healing the Stories of Your Life.*

"I am grateful that I can see how every heartbreak, every trauma, every tear has created a foundation so strong that it can never be touched. And I love how I know that even if something came along and blew it into a million pieces, that something even stronger would be built in its place.

I am grateful for the road I have travelled, and the journey I've made. It's been hard and long, treacherous and terrifying, and there were times when I wasn't sure I'd make it, times when I didn't think I had it in me to keep going. But Spirit picked me up, carrying me from the inside, and I let myself be lifted. I let myself continue down the path—sometimes kicking and screaming, but I kept going, moving forward to a better and better life.

I am grateful that in those dark and lonely times, I listened to the voice that said, "It won't always be like this" because it was right. There is more love, more goodness, more hope, and more beauty than I could ever have imagined. And I am grateful that I can see that.

Right now there is so much gratitude inside of me that I can't seem to break it down and speak to smaller parts. All I can feel is the fullness of it. How light and happy I am.

I am grateful for Tyler's little cat Velcro. For his curiosity, his mischievous ways, his guts and his innocence.

I am grateful for this sacred space in which I sit and write. Clear, pure, and holy. I can feel the presence of God the minute I open the door. Whatever stress or confusion may haunt me in the moment, I walk in here, and I feel peaceful and content—one with myself.

With so much gratitude filling the space inside me and so many things, events, situations, and people that I could speak about—I start to wonder how I can ever bring this exercise to a close. When do I stop writing? How do I finish without sounding like I just cut myself off mid-thought or mid-sentence?

Well I guess that leads me to another gratitude. I am the creator—the beginner, the middler, and the ender—of every piece. Much like in my life, I have creative license to go where I please and stop when I choose. It's simple really—and when I trust the rhythm of the process I realize that all things have a natural end. I don't have to figure it out, seize up, or try to control it. Just relax and let it flow. And for that, I am truly grateful."

Like attracts like and the Universe doesn't discern. Since what you focus on grows, focus on that which you want to see grow more abundantly in your life. Focus on what makes your heart sing. Have gratitude for all that you have and watch more and more abundance, synchronicity, and good things show up. That's simply the way it is. It's a law: The Universal Law of Attraction.

You want something—you ask and then you open to receive it. See it in your mind's eye and mostly feel how it feels to have manifested what it is you are asking for. If you don't give yourself messages that it will never come to you, expect that it will. If at your core you believe that these things happen to other people, not you, that you didn't have the education, the right parents, the right this or that to ever get ahead, well, that's a recipe to see the evidence of your belief system. You need to hold the vision of what you desire in your mind, not the reality of what's in front of you. In other words, even if you don't currently 'see' it yet, carry on living your life as if it is on its way.

Einstein said you cannot solve a problem with the same mind that created it. Instead of making the same choices over and over again, decide to change your thoughts in order to change that reality. Awareness is the first step in healing, and it's hard to go backward once you make a conscious decision to move forward.

Ask for what you want and expect it to happen because God and your angels can't wait to deliver it to you. But don't sit and look at your watch waiting for it to come. Divine timing is when it will arrive. Be the heron. Remember that patience is not empty waiting. It's inner certainty. You don't need to wait for anything. Just conjure up the state that whatever it is you want will be provided for you and bask in that state now.

Do you want more money? What is it about more money that will make you happy? Oh, it's the car you have set your eyes on that you want to drive. Good, perfect. Take yourself on an imaginary trip in your mind and see yourself cruising down the highway in it. Or picture it sitting in your driveway. Better yet, go to the car dealer and take it for a test drive and really get a true sense of how it feels to be behind the wheel. Then hold on to the feelings that driving that luxury car has given you and then let it go. That's the key. Let it go. See it, feel it, claim it, and let the object of your desire go but maintain the happy feelings it conjured up in you. And if you want to stretch even more, do it for everything in your life. Live from a state of joy and appreciation now—before you have what you think is going to provide you with happiness. Be happy now.

This is akin to what I think Gandhi meant in his famous words, "Be the change you wish to see in the world." Be that now. Carry that energy with you now. I can tell you from first-hand experience, it's this lesson that has brought me the greatest joy in my life. I don't need to wait for anything to happen. I can find things in a heartbeat that bring me joy, which begets more of the same. Writing this to you is one of those times. In Eckhart Tolle's famous book *The Power of Now*, he emphasizes that in every moment there is grace, truth, and peace.

We do not have the privilege to know what is going to happen in the course of any day. I like to think of life as a surprise party. Every day is different. Every day we get to unwrap life's gifts to us. Even when they aren't tied in a beautiful bow. We get to choose how we will respond to the situations that life delivers. If it's something we don't want and certainly didn't ask for (on a conscious level, that is), we can expend untold energy railing against it, but it's not going to make it go away. Dissing it will make it get louder and worse. Instead, you can take a deep breath, move into stillness and ask for guidance. Then listen and watch for the guidance, as it will come in many guises if you pay attention. You will be given exactly what you need in order to navigate the situation in the best way possible. You will be given messages to take the next step and the next from a calm and centred place instead of a reactionary one.

> *"May you live like a river flows carried*
> *by the surprise of its own unfolding."*
> **– John O'Dononue**

Life is here for your highest evolution. You don't get to choose it. Where free will comes in is in the way in which you respond to life. When you flow with it, knowing there is something valuable for you to learn, even if you can't figure it out at the time or can't make sense of it—or can't imagine why bad things happen when you are doing your best and have the best in mind for others—you can still decide to apply a mindful response to what comes in order to flow with the river instead of traverse more and more rapids, a.k.a unrelenting drama.

Life will be life. Living on earth is not always easy. It is filled with challenges, and it is our job to find the ways we can be the eye in the storm. To be the lighthouse that will bring ourselves and others safely back to shore.

It is from this inner state of being that you want to write your memoir, for it is here, in this mind-set that you will give the best of you to the words you will deliver.

In this chapter, you were able to deepen the voice that originates in your soul. This is the you that no matter what you have done or not done, knows you are worthy, worthwhile, loved, loveable, and loving. And it is from this truth and inner knowledge that you are valuing your life, your stories, and your ability to write your stories from a place of honour. Congratulations. This is the voice that will leave you loving not only what you write and the legacy you leave but also your life right here, right now. And that is the aim for all of us. To live in today with appreciation, joy, and gratitude, honouring our divinity as well as our humanness and being a light to the world by simply showing up as we are.

Chapter 6

Looking Back to Grow Forward: Gifts and Lessons

Step 3

When you choose love and forgiveness, you take the high road. You live your true divine purpose.

Step 3 offers up the awesome gifts that await you as you rewrite the painful stories from the past; coming into harmony with yourself and the world—and with the truth of who you really are beyond your ego mind, beyond the pain, regrets, and fears. You move beyond the stories that have held you back to reengage with the joyous, creative, and spiritual being that you really are.

Here you consciously choose your spiritual essence to integrate with your humanness to bring the presence of divinity into your daily life. You no longer relate to your past as just things that happened to you. Instead you carry the key that opens the lock to a treasure trove of new understanding, growth, peace, and acceptance. Writing your memoir from this heightened awareness gets energetically transmitted to your readers.

When you take the position that everything that's happened to you has happened for a reason, you can become the observer and witness to your stories. You are no longer the victim of circumstance. You recognize that Universal intelligence and guidance has been there with you and for you in every moment.

We become detectives, sleuths, and anthropologists—excavating that which has been buried or hidden. We become social scientists, observing our behavior, manners, attitudes, and actions that have helped shape our lives. We see what has been effective and what hasn't.

In this step, you come nose to nose with the fact that it is a privilege to be alive. You break the cycle of mediocrity knowing every breath that you are given is a gift. When you build your life on this foundation, you can expect to be blessed with everyday miracles.

My Story Rewritten: From Victim to Victory!

Years ago, a miracle occurred when I awoke out of a coma. I came to know, unequivocally, that my life is sacred.

I was ready to set down the label of bipolar as I am not my pathology or my diagnosis.

I am a loving, caring, and kind person with an illness. When it reaches a certain level of chemical imbalance, I cannot control it—in spite of popular belief that if I tried harder or really wanted to and applied myself, I could. To a certain extent that is true, but for me—when it crosses over a certain undetermined line—it has a mind and a momentum of its own, and it doesn't matter how much therapy I do or yoga or affirmations or anything else; I can't seem to stop it, and eventually the torture chamber in my mind with its unrelenting voices saying I should just end it all has caused me to take those drastic steps on five different occasions.

When I was ready to let go of the names that I have heard people with mental health challenges called—cuckoo, nuts, crazy, dysfunctional, beyond hope (which were not only from outsiders but also, on my worst days, me)—I finally said, "Enough." I ended the barrage of negative internal comments that made me feel bad about myself and chose to love myself instead. On that day, I reclaimed my life and have never looked back.

In fact, that is when my mental illness became my gift to myself and to everyone around me.

What stories do you carry that at first felt like a nightmare to you but, in retrospect, you can see how they have offered you some of your life's greatest gifts and lessons? How do those stories serve you now? In what ways have you grown because of them? What did you specifically learn from these circumstances and how have they served others in your life?

My experiences with bipolar illness have given me much greater compassion and insight into not only my own situation but also those of others who walk a similar path. Is this the case for you as well? Do you see how your set of circumstances and what it has taught you has made you more conscious of people who also struggle with similar challenges? Are you actively helping those people? Do you have a desire to? These are simply questions for reflection. There are no right or wrong answers. Do you know that simply by recognizing the gifts that have come out of these difficult events for you and choosing to live the high road, you already emit an energy frequency that is benefiting humanity? Every time we heal, we not only heal ourselves, but we also heal everyone in our wake, and that becomes a pebble in a vast pond where the ripples of healing go on and on and on. Now how about that for motivation to heal and write your memoir from your empowered self. Just think about the countless people whose lives will transform because you had the courage to write your stories.

Albert Einstein said we can live our life as though nothing is a miracle or as though everything is a miracle. Let's choose the path of awe, of miracles, of wonder, the eyes of a curious child ready to touch, taste, feel, and know everything there is to know about. Even though you and I have lived so much of our lives already and we can't change the events that happened to us, looking back through the eyes of wonder brings in a whole new meaning. Living from this place is exhilarating.

Every experience gives us an opportunity to express love or fear, peace or strife.

As you know, when you carry celebratory energy, it is infectious. People want to be around you, and you attract the kinds of people you want to have in your life. And what's more, you get to share with them why a broken leg, or a divorce, or being laid off a job was the turning point, the catalyst for something so much greater.

Often when we go through traumatic events, we are just so happy to be on the other side of them that we don't go back and reflect about what we actually did to help us get through that time.

Now, while you are writing your memoir, there is no better time to determine what tools you have acquired in your tool kit that have kept you in good stead because those are the kinds of things you will want to share with others.

The following are true examples of what some of my clients have acknowledged as the gifts and lessons they received from their healthy choices. Perhaps some of these will apply to you or trigger others that you can identify.

- Learned to create good boundaries
- Learned to forgive
- Learned to love
- Learned to let go
- Learned I am more afraid than I thought but willing to learn how to trust
- Learned I can open to spirituality
- Learned I have talent
- Learned how being closed, angry, and unwilling to change or forgive has stolen years from my life
- Learned I have choice
- Learned to open my fists of fear and paralysis to let a butterfly land
- Learned to be compassionate with myself
- Learned to like myself
- Learned I am great in an emergency
- Learned from writing my stories that I have had an interesting life—not any easy one but one worth recording and leaving to my children

- Learned that I wish I knew then what I know now but it is still not too late
- Learned to cherish today
- Learned to have gratitude for everything—it's all a fascinating story
- Learned not to take myself so seriously
- Learned to have a sense of humour
- Learned that as soon as I finally let go in my mind and heart of the man I was holding on to, I would meet the man of my dreams.
- Learned to have faith
- Learned how to adapt to change
- Learned I could stick with something until the end
- Learned discernment—knowing when to quit
- Learned I am way stronger than I thought
- Learned I am intelligent, capable, and a quick study
- Learned I was wrong about who I thought I was.
- Learned I am worthy of a beautiful life and capable of cocreating one.
- Learned to focus on what's important and what isn't—to not sweat the small stuff.

- Learned that it is up to me to make my life better

Writing Exercise: Opening to the Gifts and Lessons of Your Life Stories

Mark the gifts and lessons from the examples above that you relate to the most as well as identify your own and begin to write the stories that offered you these gifts and lessons. One story at a time. Stay with it until it feels complete. Honour the details of it.

Who else was involved? How did your life change as a result of this experience? Take your time remembering and relating these stories. There is no need to rush. You can start off with just ideas that inform your choices and later, as more information comes to you, add it to the story. Or, if one of the gifts calls an experience to you when you put pen to paper, the entire story tumbles out, absolutely go with it.

Below are two true-to-life accounts. The first one is written by a former memoir-writing student and the second story is my own. They are examples of rewriting memories with the intention of healing heartbreak, sadness and pain in order to find "the crack, the crack that is in everything. That's where the light comes in," to quote Leonard Cohen in his famous song, "Anthem." We wrote them knowing the writing would be a major key to catharsis leading to empowerment.

By staying true to our intention, courage, and commitment, the same processes that I outline in this book, each story shows how we were rewarded by the Universe in ways that began with a dream that originated in our hearts. By hanging on to the reigns of our dreams, following our inner guidance, and living Einstein's words, as though everything was a miracle and therefore expecting goodness to follow, it absolutely did. And then, what followed next was the inspiration to write the story of transformation as part of our memoir.

This is what awaits you as well. The rewards of rewriting your stories so that you can live today with meaning, inner peace, joy, and grace. Here is where you discover your sweet spot.

I trust the following stories will inspire you. Although the circumstances will be different than yours, the inner journey taken is the same. And this, I feel, is the heart of our humanity.

These Hands by Marya Nijland

Looking at my old wrinkled hands, my thoughts are floating far away to my beginnings…

These hands were playing with my dark brown bear, the only toy I really loved. I used to carry him around the house and tucked him in bed with me such a long time ago. What a feeling of gratitude for the safety and love I received when I was so vulnerable and fragile.

These hands stroked my little brother who was born in August of 1945 when I was 7 years old and who came after my first brother had died on March 31st of that year. That baby was so treasured by all of us and especially by me.

These hands explored… in my teenage years. There were several exciting sexual discoveries. I felt alive and full of adventure… throughout my life my hands were my sexual tools.

These hands learned to write stories and essays in High School. They were helpers to my inner thoughts.

These hands made love to the four people I have sexually loved in my life. My heart fills with joy and gratitude, still at this moment.

These hands were folded in prayers and meditations over and over in rough times and times of gratitude.

These hands played the harmonium as a child and now in later life they are touching the black and whites of my beloved piano helping me to compose new melodies, a new found love.

These hands have known poverty, rolled up pennies and dimes, wondering how to make ends meet. Now, having no financial worries, I am so grateful that I am able to help others now and then.

These hands still stroke my husband's old beautiful face with his funny little beard. There is no better face in this whole wide world than his. I am so grateful to have such a great companion.

These hands have made fists to demand justice for human rights, equality and freedom. They have expressed anger and frustration. Now these fists have straightened out to hands that make banners and write letters of protest. I am grateful that I can make a difference.

These hands were made for writing, crafting, baking, making music and above all loving and holding hands with people here and all over this world. And they reach out to hug my friends as they enter our front door.

I am thoroughly grateful and if I die tomorrow, I hope these friends will say:

"Marya—she was a woman who said YES to life."

One of my earliest inspirations came from James Kavanagh, in his book of poetry written in 1970, *There Are Men Too Gentle to Live among Wolves*.

Relating to his poem, I wondered how I would navigate my life when I was hopelessly depressed. I was twenty at the time, and my best friend since grade two, Suki, and I had just ended our friendship. Actually, she ended it, and I felt like my life was over.

James Kavanagh's poem helped me to know I was not alone.

> *"To those who can hear the honking of geese, above the sound of traffic, who can hear the weeping of boys above the sound of mortars, who refuse to take life as it is, because it wasn't always.*
>
> *We searchers are ambitious only for life itself, for everything beautiful it can provide. We are like forests and mountains, deserts and hidden rivers, and the lonely cities as well. Our sadness is as much a part of our lives as is our laughter. To share our sadness with one we love is perhaps as great a joy as we can know—unless it be we share our laughter.*
>
> *Most of all we want to love and be loved. We want to live in a relationship that will not impede our wandering, nor prevent our search, nor lock us in prison walls, that will take us for what little we have to give. We do not want to prove ourselves to another nor compete for our lives.*
>
> *This is for wanderers, dreamers and lovers—for lonely men and women who dare to ask of life everything good and beautiful.*
>
> *It is for those who are too gentle to live among wolves."*
>
> **– James Kavanagh**

Here is what I wrote years after Suki and I parted ways.

> *"She enters my thoughts out of nowhere and suddenly I'm consumed by that familiar longing again—a crippling emptiness that has all the scars of a motherless child—vainly searching shadowed street corners for the one who's never, ever coming back. I suppose I'll go to my grave with this. Therapy and the years have played their bit in assisting to dull the ache*

but it comes back anyway. It comes back in torrents and floods and then ebbs away again leaving me like the darkened streets, desolate and bare.

And again someday, when I least expect to remember—when I'm doing something menial like ironing a shirt or crossing a street or thinking about buying myself flowers—she'll return in full life-size form and dimensions, equipped with sounds and tastes and smells and the movie projector is running on automatic and we're children again, running in the park and giggling over some silly joke or about one of the teachers at school. The secrets. We told each other all our secrets and shared all of our dreams for what we wanted when we grew up. We shared it all. Teenage tears and fears and the excitement over a new boy. And we sang. How we loved to sing. We knew all the words to every song. "Smile" was ours. And we did everything together. Best friends. We were best friends. Blood sisters. Didn't we cut our index fingers until they bled when we were eight, then rubbed them together and swore an oath to never, ever part. It worked. She lives inside my veins. It's only in the other world she ceases to exist—the one that shows its face to the others. But the one who lives inside and peaks out only now and again is the one who remembers and she's the one who misses you, Suki. She's the one who wishes more than anything else in this entire life that you would come back and love her again."

Addendum: I am delighted to tell you she did come back. I initiated contact forty-three years later. Yes, that's right—almost half a century later I friended her on Facebook. She responded immediately. I flew the three thousand miles back to Toronto, and we reunited with a life force as though our lives depended on it. We recounted what happened. Neither story matched and we didn't care. Our hearts were intact. We walked the streets of our youth and remembered the people who were part of it, and we laughed and sang our song, "Smile," and have been smiling ever since.

You may have noticed that these stories are written in different styles. Poetry, prose, as it was happening in the moment, or looking back. Each style is perfect for it reflects the uniqueness of the writer.

It is not necessarily in the writing itself that the gifts and lessons of that life event are revealed to us. Do not be surprised if this is what you experience. Setting the intention for shifting your thoughts towards things that happened in the past will set up the conditions for you to see the results of this in exactly the right time. Divine time. Know all is well.

> *"Patience is not empty waiting, it is inner certainty."*
> **– Alman**

 Time to Write: What has your pain come to teach you?

Your turn. Looking back, what lessons and gifts have your life stories brought to you?

Once again, gather your journal, a pen, and a glass of water. Give yourself at least one hour of uninterrupted time as you write down what you have identified as some of your strengths as well as the gifts and lessons you have learned through some of the painful experiences of the past.

Consider what lessons these circumstances taught you about yourself. Looking back, what did you learn? How can these same circumstances be gifts that enliven you? How might you express that new awareness to others facing a similar situation to yours?

These tuned-in assessments can happen after every story you write or at another time when you are out gardening or taking a shower or ironing a shirt. Often when we are not thinking about something but have set the intention to know, answers and ah-has come unbidden.

You may even find that there is a common theme running through most of your stories. There may be one particular story where you have derived the biggest gifts and ah-has.

This is exciting sleuth work. It is here that you start to recognize how far you have come and how many strengths you possibly took for granted. You will need to take them into account now that you want to recount them in your memoir.

For me, the greatest gifts were as a result of living with bipolar illness. I would never have believed that at the time. However, in a final-straw moment, realizing that what I called the torture chamber of my mind was too much for me to carry, I surrendered my pain to the Universe. I was on my knees willing to do whatever it took to rise above the unrelenting anxiety and suicidal ruminations. I was shocked that the answer I was given was to write a book or play and tell my story. That was a huge leap when I had kept that secret from everyone other than my family and closest friends. Eventually, still shaking in my boots, I said yes. Writing *Madness, Masks and Miracles* gave me new meaning, drive and purpose.

The gift in taking that action was complete liberation from the shame I carried to becoming a strong mental health advocate, a spokesperson for hope. Currently I am executing a dream whose time has come. It's an organization called Academy for Creative and Healing Arts (ACHA), for people with mental health challenges.

It's about the power of creative expression to transform mental illness into mental health. Yes, when we heal ourselves, the gifts we give others are immeasurable. And then they come back to us one thousand-fold. You can read more about ACHA on my website: https://junieswadron.com/mental-health/

A dear friend of mine, Kath, asked me if I thought she should show the DVD of my play to her eighty-year-old mother, who has bipolar illness. She shared that her mother's illness affected the whole family, but no one has ever spoken about it. It was always the elephant in the room, but no one dared say a word.

Kath, along with her mom's youngest sister, Marie, decided it was best to show the play to her mom. They watched it together. The next day, her mother said to her, "Kath, it's the first time in my life, I know it wasn't my fault." For eighty long years, guilt ravaged Kath's mom, Mary. She believed it was her fault—that she must have done something purposeful that caused her family's suffering because she didn't know how to stop the depressions or the highs while they were happening even though she wanted to with all her heart. It was her unbearable shame that kept her from ever broaching the subject.

Even now, as I write this, I get a lump in my throat because it was for this reason that I stayed the course of writing and producing my play. Now, with Kath's mom's new awareness that she was not the cause of her illness nor her family's pain, there was an opening to discuss what each of their experiences had been like.

Within just days of Kath telling me that story, I was introduced to a woman through a mutual friend. We saw that we had a common friend on Facebook. When I told her that he emceed a play I wrote several years ago. She told me she was there in the audience.

"What?" I said. "No way."

"Oh, but that's not all," she continued. "That play was the catalyst for me to turn my life around. I had no idea what it was about. My friend invited me, and I just went along. While watching it, I wanted to bolt, get out of that auditorium, but my friend wouldn't let me. Instead, when it was over, I made a solemn oath to myself to turn my life around as I was going in a bad direction. I stayed true to my oath, and today my life doesn't look anything like it did back then."

I told her she had no idea of the gift she gave me by telling me this story. It validated why I went the distance when I wanted to quit a million times. Producing it was fraught with frustration and challenges, yet I kept going because I knew that message had to be heard. It was no longer just about me. I had to move beyond my own fear so that perhaps even one person's life would be changed by it.

The same is possible with your memoir. It could also impact someone's life or many people's lives that you may never know about, and that is a beautiful motivation to write it.

 Time to Write: Who Are Your Mentors?

Who have some of your mentors been? People who have influenced you the most, helped you move through trying times? What was it about them that inspired you? What qualities did they possess? How did they specifically help you?

In the following writing exercise, choose just one person who has been a teacher or mentor for you. Allow the memory prompts to trigger the specifics of your encounter and the effect he or she had on your life.

Give yourself at least one hour of uninterrupted time. Fetch your journal, a pen, and a glass of water and begin.

Has there been someone in your life who impacted it in such a way as to make it easier, gentler, better, or somewhat kinder? Someone who took the time to be with you and uplift you so you were able to look at the world with fresh eyes? If so, imagine that person in front of you now and begin to recall the day that you first met.

How old were you? What is his or her name? What were the conditions in which you met? Did you like each other from the start or was it a relationship that grew over time? How long was this person in your life? Is he or she still in it? What was it that made your relationship particularly meaningful or special? What were some of this person's qualities that meant the most to you? And now consider some of the specific ways he or she influenced your life. What did he or she do or say that made a difference? How did your thinking, behaviour or attitudes change as a result of his or her motivation?

If that person had not entered your life, do you think you would be the same today? If no, why not? In what ways do you think you would be different? What were you like before you met? What path did that person's influence put you on that you may not have chosen otherwise? Have you been able to pass some of what you learned on to others? And since we are all teachers and students at the same time, in what ways do you think you may have influenced or benefited your mentor? What truth or awareness did you bring to him or her?

Is this person still alive today? If so, have you considered thanking him or her for the life-altering gifts you were given? We never know for certain how people feel about themselves. Receiving a letter of appreciation, thanking and acknowledging them by sharing how they made a positive difference in our lives could be the thing they need to bring about a renewed sense of hope, peace, joy, or well-being. Consider finding out where this person is today and offering your heartfelt appreciation, possibly even through this story you're about to write. And now allow your heart to open to the wonder and splendor of the Universe—how Providence sends us remarkable people to help guide us and show us the way just in the nick of time.

Sometimes they come for just a day or a month or a year, but their impact lasts a lifetime. It is grace that brings these people to us. If you have been fortunate enough to have had such a person in your life, then wrap yourself in gratitude and feel the love enfold you. Consider writing your mentor a letter. Even if he or she has since passed, it is both healing and gratifying to do this. Love moves beyond the veil. Your grateful energy is being sent.

Imagine your memoir doing exactly this for someone else or in fact, most likely, countless others. And even if you choose to write it for your children or grandchildren so that they will know you better, what a beautiful legacy you will give and example you will set.

I have written a letter to a true teacher and mentor. Her name was Davida Hoyos and she was a friend in every sense of the word. You will find her story in Appendix C.

Chapter 7

Structuring Your Life Stories— The Road Map

Step 4

T ake a deep breath because everything is outlined for you here. I take out all the guesswork to help you write your memoir with ease, grace, and joy. If you have been doing the writing exercises that have been laid out in prior chapters, you already know how. Of all the guidelines on how to write memoir that I will teach you, the most important one of all is to tap into your heart and write from that place. Here you will access your authentic voice and highest good which will set you on a path to freedom.

And to assist you further, here are many guidelines to take out the guesswork. Some of the following processes will resonate more than others. Choose the ones that speak to you, as there are many ways to get there. I have tried to be as comprehensive as possible, anticipating questions you might have. However, if your stories gush out of you, you don't need to go back to see if you are "doing it right." You are doing it right for the creative process. Much later, when you wish to read back with a more discerning eye, you can. However, when your writing flows, when your stories simply "write themselves" don't interrupt yourself with needing to know what's working and what isn't. Simply allow.

The tools: A desk or kitchen table; computer, paper, or journal; pen; and a glass of water.

Creating a Sacred Space

There's nothing like having an inviting, friendly, beautiful writing space to inspire you every day. It doesn't have to be big, just welcoming. Make it personal. Make it yours. Light a candle. Bring out your favourite incense. Bring in colourful flowers, precious stones, shells you collected on the beach, crystals, a favourite prayer or affirmation, or anything else that will make your writing space special. You may want to put a photo on your writing desk or next to your computer of a special person or pet and imagine them smiling at you as you write. (Pets do too smile.)

Or conversely, you may want to keep it simple and not have anything in your space. For some, having special items may be distracting.

Also, tell your family what you are doing and ask them to please respect your new writing area and that the books, photo albums, and letters you placed there are not be touched.

Respect and embrace your sacred space.

Organization

I have found the best way to keep organized is to keep everything in a three-ring binder or folder so your writing is all under one cover rather than using loose sheets that could get lost.

Make sure you number your pages. Use separate tabs for each life story. Also keep separate folders or large envelopes that you label for each story to create order with any memorabilia you are collecting such as photographs or family documents you wish to include.

Computer or Handwritten

As to whether to handwrite or use the computer, do whatever you're most comfortable with. The benefit of the computer is that later, after your story is written, it makes it much easier to go back and make changes. You can cut and paste and delete or add without any difficulty.

If you are using the computer, be aware of distractions like surfing the net and checking emails. Getting started, or the first fifteen minutes after you sit down to write, is critical to your success.

During your designated writing time, to help reduce distractions, commit to not surfing the net or checking your emails. If you have a way of turning off your internet connection, do it. Unplug your phone. Make sure you are not hungry before you start writing. Keep a bottle of water at your writing table.

Keep a Journal as an Adjunct to Writing Your Memoir

Often there are feelings that come up while you are writing your memoir that trigger emotional responses. In the worst-case scenario, they could stop you from writing. You might leave the computer and eat a chocolate bar instead or get angry at some innocent bystander that says, "Please hand me my glasses." You may shout, "Get up and get them yourself!|" Before that happens, as soon as you see strong feelings surface as you are writing your story and they are tampering with what you want to put in your memoir, get out your trusty journal and say everything (the truth) that's on your mind. You are at a crossroads and a prime healing opportunity. Give yourself some spaciousness and tenderness. When you come back to writing that same story in your memoir, you will have much more clarity, stability and wisdom.

You Do Not Have to Be a Great Writer

You don't need to be an accomplished writer to write your memoir. You don't need to have taken writing courses, have a certificate or degree in writing, or any other such thing. You just need to be able to be honest and write from your heart.

Let go of perfectionism, spelling, punctuation, grammar, and having to do it "right." Instead, drop into your belly and try not to think about the writing at all. When you are thinking, you are judging, planning, or figuring out what to say next. This writing process calls for stepping out of your own way and not editing as you write.

It is about being fully in your body, allowing memories to flow from your head to your heart to your hand and on to the page.

Marion Woodman, in an interview in Common Boundary, said, "After much thought, I realized the trouble I had writing that bleak Friday afternoon was due to my approach. I was trying to analyze, trying to explain rationally. I was failing miserably because I was approaching the task through my head. I had to drop into my belly."

Nathalie Goldberg, in Writing Down the Bones, states, "In writing, when you are truly on, there's no writer, no paper, no pen. No thoughts. Only writing does writing—everything else is gone."

Your Writing Style

You are unique and there is no right or wrong way to write your stories. Perhaps some of your stories want to come out as letters or fairy tales. Be true to your own method of writing. Even if you have never written poetry before, stay with it if that is how it emerges. Trust and enjoy the process.

Breathing

Writing is a full-bodied exercise. It is not just the brain and the fingers. It calls for full breath. When you get scared, your breathing becomes shallow and so does your writing.

The more grounded you are in your body, the deeper your writing becomes. When you are breathing from a shallow place, your writing tends to stay on the surface. Breathe from deep in your belly and write from that place.

In his book, *Writing from the Body*, John Lee explains, "To begin writing with the full power of our body's knowledge, we must welcome our life, our breath and our emotions completely. Write whatever bursts forward from the breath. Let the pen follow where the breath leads. We have only to begin breathing fully to show life that we are serious about embracing her."

Making Time to Write

It's best to get into a routine. Find an uninterrupted space of time to write every day, preferably at the same time. If you can't do it every day, perhaps it's possible to write once, twice, or three times a week. Whatever works for you, mark it on your calendar and commit to it. Then, turn off your telephone. Share with family members what you are doing so they know to be respectful of your writing time.

If you need to, reread *The Healing Power of Intention, The Healing Power of Courage*, and *The Healing Power of Commitment* to help you get started. Also carry a notebook with you to write down ideas that come to you during the day so you will remember them when you sit down at your desk to write.

Ways to Stay Grounded

Although writing one's life can be exhilarating when recapturing beautiful memories or coming to terms and moving through to the other side of painful ones, it can also catapult you into feeling like your entire emotional foundation is collapsing. It is vital to stay grounded and safe by taking special care to nurture yourself throughout this process.

Consider all the tools you have used throughout your life that keep you resilient and sane. What is it you usually do that works, that keeps you resilient? Tapping? Meditation? Practice whatever self-care you need as you traverse past painful memories. Make sure you eat well, drink plenty of water, and get enough exercise, fresh air, and sleep. Refuel your sense of humour. Rent a funny movie. Reach out. Call a friend. Dance. Go for a walk in nature. Meditate. Keep an attitude of gratitude. Breathe deeply. Read inspirational writings or prayers. Give whatever you are going through over to God/Divine Intelligence/Creator. If you remember and record painful events from times past, remember it is part of your past. You survived it and are on the other side of it now. Bring yourself back to this day, this moment, for it is right here, right now that you are safe. Use conscious breath to do this. Breathe deeply and often.

Treat your pages as your dearest friend, one who is ready and willing to accept you as you are. Remember not to judge yourself or your writing when you put pen to paper (or keyboard).

"My past is nothing more than the trail that I have left behind. What drives my life today is the energy that I generate in each of my present moments."

– Wayne Dyer

Right Brain versus Left Brain Process

Memoir writing engages a process that calls for right brain activity, which uses pictures, symbols, and images and is nonverbal. It is the part of our nature that is intuitive, sensuous, artistic, and spontaneous. It works with shapes and patterns. While writing, simply be open to receive. You are a conduit, not a planner. As stated earlier, you write without paying attention to spelling, grammar, or punctuation. This is what the left brain function does. It is verbal, linear, logical, rational, and cognitive. This is the part of the brain you want to engage in if you decide to go back and edit. It is not for now.

Mind Mapping

Mind mapping is a fast, fun, and effective way to remember the details of your story before you start writing. It is a great way to bring back memories and access your right brain through word association. It's brainstorming on the page.

Instead of writing down lists, which are linear, draw a circle in the middle of your notebook. Draw lines coming out of the centre circle to other circles or bubbles. In those bubbles write the first words that pop into your head. If those words trigger another thought, draw a line to another circle and write the thought. It is an excellent tool to help access the memories of these events. The main circle can become your theme or chapter title and the spokes of it are the meat of the story that goes inside. In the example below, you will see in the large circle in the middle, the name of this book *Your Life Matters* In your

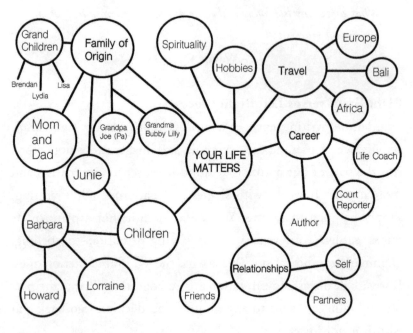

middle circle, you can write "My Story" or if you have a working title, you can put it there. Then add the spokes and bubbles that are relevant to your life.

What to Do on Designated Writing Day

I suggest you use the following centring exercise if, for example, you arrive at your writing table in distress after a busy day or simply have lots of things on your mind. This exercise will help calm and relax you before you begin to write. I have suggested this exercise in my book, *Re-Write Your Life*, and there is an audio recording of it on my website that you can download if you would like to hear it rather than read it. https://junieswadron.com/products-and-services/re-write-your-life-book/

Centring Exercise

Get comfortable in your chair and begin to focus on your breath. Take some deep breaths in from your belly and let go. As you exhale, let go of tension and worry. Let go of any thoughts that you have. Let go of anything that is preventing you from being here right now and breathe. Gently bring yourself into this moment.

With every new breath, breathe in joy and peace. Breathe out tension or worry. With every breath, you move into a deeper state of relaxation. Breathe. Now scan your body. Notice where you are carrying tension. Next imagine your breath moving into those places to release and soften, fully letting go. You are becoming more relaxed with every breath you take.

Now in your mind's eye, take yourself somewhere in nature where your spirit feels at home—somewhere you have either been before or somewhere your imagination takes you to for the first time. Go there with all your inner senses fully alive and awake. Breathe in the beauty of this natural setting. Notice what you see in front of you. Observe all the details. Notice what you see in the distance. Slowly turn and look in all directions. Notice what time of day it is. Are you at a beach or in a forest? Somewhere else, perhaps?

Listen to the sounds. Is there an ocean, a river, a creek near you, a meadow? What sounds do you hear? What colours do you see? Breathe. Notice how good you feel in this beautiful place. Every time you come here, you will feel better and better. This is your safe place. Your own inner sanctuary. This is the place of letting go of all worldly concerns. Here there is nothing you have to do, no where you have to go, and no one you have to please.

Allow yourself to be fully present to all that is around you. In this exquisite inner sanctuary, this place of beauty and stillness, you can simply be. You feel renewed here. You are happy and at peace.

Enjoy your time here. Know that this is your spiritual sanctuary and yours to come home to whenever you choose. It will always be here waiting for you. A place of stillness, outside of personal and worldly concerns and where you can reconnect with your Higher Self. This is a sacred place where you join with Universal love and intelligence and bathe in a radiant sea of golden light and love. Take another deep breath and let go.

When you are ready, you can come back to your sacred writing space, relaxed, renewed, and prepared to begin to write your story.

Invocation—Opening to the Gifts

St. Francis affirms the following:

"It is in giving that we receive,

"In pardoning, we are pardoned,
"And in surrendering, we are born to eternal life."

The following invocation is to be used before writing any story that holds pain, grief, fear, shame, sorrow, regret, anger, hostility, or resentment. The invocation will help you let go of all that no longer serves you by allowing yourself to be held in the hands of God. (You may substitute the word God with any other name that feels more comfortable for you—e.g., Light, Universal Intelligence, Love, the Creator, or Spirit). You can also find the audio version of this invocation at https://junieswadron.com/products-and-services/re-write-your-life-book/.

Invocation

As I prepare to write the following life story, I let go and let God. I am open and willing to receive the highest truth with respect to all that has happened to me. I acknowledge and accept that the people and circumstances in my life were brought to me for my learning, healing, and growth.

I am open to the gifts that the people and circumstances in this story offered me. I receive these gifts easily, graciously, and with gratitude. I am letting go of any negative thinking that would cause me to deny the blessings that this life story offers. As I write my truth, I open to receive complete healing.

I take ownership and responsibility for the choices I have made. I love and forgive myself for any choices that hurt me and/or others. I am also ready and willing to forgive those who I perceive hurt me in any way. I am willing to see the innocence in myself and in them. I take a deep breath in and let go of any fear or tension I may be carrying.

I open to Universal Grace and Intelligence, helping to restore any imbalances for my highest good. Through the writing and remembering of this story and appreciation for the inherent gifts that were offered, I open to returning to a state of deep peace, health, and joy. I remember that everything I have experienced is for my soul's growth and evolution. I breathe in light and love. I give thanks as I begin to write and remember [name your story; e.g., "The Story of My First Husband, Fred"].

Write Your Story from Wherever Your Energy Is

You can write chronologically or thematically. If you choose to write your memoir from the time of your birth to your present age, know that with the help of the mind map, you can choose whatever stories you wish to write and then put them in order of dates later. The same is true for themes—such as a graduation or a death of a loved one or a significant move in your life. Write where your energy is, not where you think you should go next. If, in the last writing session you shared about how your aunt Ethel's unconditional love for you had a huge impact on your life and have since thought of more you want to include, of course, go for it. However, if you are more inspired to write about your trip to Italy as a teenager, go for that. You can return to the story of your auntie Ethel later. When we write where our energy is, it will flow. If not, we will be thinking of the other things we would rather be writing. Just write them instead.

Keep a Journal While Writing Your Life Stories

While writing your life stories, you still have a present-day life. It's wise to carry a journal and write about anything that comes up that could be triggered by your writing and possibly affect how you respond to others during this time. Write the truth in your journal so that you can move to the other side of whatever is going on. My journal has been my best friend throughout my life because it gives me a safe place to honour my truth in the moment when I need to when it may be either unsafe, inappropriate, or simply not necessary to share what's going on for me with others. When I state the truth without embellishing or denying it, I find I release what is needed—anger, shame, fear, resentment, and confusion—and I inevitably feel better. It doesn't always happen in the moment I am writing. But the writing of it has shifted the energy around, and within a little time, I feel lighter and more spacious and most often with new understanding and awareness that I couldn't see before.

Choosing Whether to Publish Your Stories

Many people want to write their life stories but wonder whether they should publish them. It is a personal decision, and you don't need to make up your mind at the outset. Perhaps you want to write your stories for your family—to leave a legacy for your children and grandchildren.

I recommend that the first writing draft is for you alone. That way you don't have to change the names or worry about hurting people. You can write your stories the way you remember them and then later decide what you wish to leave in, change, or publish.

Writing for your benefit is not only truly liberating. It also allows you to write in an unrestricted manner, which will take you to the other side, where catharsis awaits you. After you have written these stories just for you, then you can decide whether or not you wish to publish them or even keep them in your memoir whether you publish or not. Your insights could possibly encourage, comfort, or inspire others. Many of my clients started out thinking their memoir would be for their family members only, but as they became more confident in their voice and realized how what they learned in their life could serve others, their book took on a different shape. They published and used their book as a vehicle to reach more people and gave talks as well. You can watch the video testimonial of one of my authors, Lawrence Cooper, describe how that was for him here: https://www.youtube.com/watch? v=luD45YzogH0&t=122s

In my initial writing of my books *Re-Write Your Life* and *Write Where You Are*, I included certain stories from my past, but when I published, I withdrew them because I wasn't ready to have the public know that part of my life yet. That option is open to you too. You get to decide which stories you wish to include and which ones you do not. You can write them and then take them out later if you want. This is your book, your legacy, and your freedom to choose.

I believe that everything in my life has happened for a reason. Perceived wrongdoings have been great teachers. They have helped me grow stronger and provided an opportunity to forgive and offer understanding and compassion to myself and others. The writing process has provided a vehicle that offered a safe place for my thoughts and feelings.

To publish is a personal choice, and there is no right or wrong answer.

If you wish to publish your memoir and are concerned about how people may react, there are ways around it. You can change the names of the people involved, or you can write under a pseudonym. You can also choose to write a novel and use true-to-life circumstances as part of the characters and events in the book. Of course, that changes it from being a memoir to a work of fiction but if your intention is the writing process itself, and what you personally will learn from it, then this is a wonderful option to take.

In my previous books, when I was relating circumstances that included others, I was clear that the events in the stories are my perception only and not necessarily the perception of the other people involved. Their version of how things happened may be different from my own. It's like watching a movie with a friend, discussing it afterwards, and having completely different takes on what you saw. You may recall in my story about Suki, when we met decades after the argument that initially ended our friendship, our memory of what happened was completely different. By that time, neither of us cared to be right. We were choosing to be happy instead!

Pick and Choose What's Right for You

Although there are many guidelines or tools of the trade for writing your life stories outlined in this chapter, choose the ones that feel best for you. For instance, if you are someone who likes to spend a full day writing as opposed to carving out an hour every morning with coffee before your scheduled appointments, do that. Or if you like to have your writing area filled with crystals and essential oils and pictures of loved ones smiling at you as you write, then don't hesitate. This is your time. This is your process, and whatever you can do to make it as enjoyable as possible, choose to do it. Sometimes I like to write in complete silence. In fact, it was what I thought I needed. I completely surprised myself when I wrote 80 percent of my first book, *Re-Write Your Life*, in a coffee shop. Every now and then, I'd look up and think, "Wow, is it ever noisy in here. When did all these people arrive?" The next thing I knew, I was back writing my story and found the words flowing out of me. I blew that theory of needing silence right out of the water. Feel free to experiment with the suggestions above so that you can make it fun and inviting. After all, these are your life stories, and you should honour them in each and every way you can, not just in the writing but in the process as well.

Chapter 8

How Deep Do I Dive (Part A)?

Step 5

I t is my guess that up until now you have straddled both sides of
the fence thinking about which stories to include in your book.
This step helps you clarify which one is for you at this time.

One side of the fence is filled with all the stories that warm
your heart, that make you feel good—the birthdays, anniversaries,
promotions, births of children and grandchildren, rites of passage
such as a confirmation or a bar mitzva or bat mitzvah or becoming a
Mason. Perhaps these include the day you were initiated into Wicca
or were celebrated for your years of volunteer service or the time you

back packed around Europe as a hippy in the sixties or a more recent trip to India or Machu Picchu opening you to experiences that have deepened your spiritual practices.

On the other side of the fence are all the stories that run the gambit from unpleasant to making you want to throw up at the thought of recounting them. It's scary for you to think of writing about them because they were hard enough to live through once. Yet, although they are the stories you'd sooner forget, you choose to write about them. You recognize you are making this choice in order to learn, heal, grow, and be set free from the painful past at last. You also know you have many tools in your "how to move through difficult times and be resilient" toolbox. I have many as well that I will share with you in the next chapter, "How Deep Do I Dive (Part B)."

It doesn't mean if you choose to write your celebratory stories now you can't choose the stories you wish to heal that are outlined in Chapter 6.

In this chapter, we will focus on Part A, your feel-good stories.

You are quite pleased to just write these for now, and in fact it is exciting to thinking about recalling and scribing these special moments in time. The following writing exercise offers you a series of memory prompts to help bring the details of these memories up close.

If you come to your writing table with lots on your mind, I recommend you read the Centring Exercise in Chapter 7. It will help bring you back into the here and now feeling tranquil, relaxed, and ready to write.

Or if you are relatively relaxed already, simply use the directives in the following guided visualization. But first, I have a fun mind map exercise to help you identify the special events in your life you wish to include in your memoir.

There are probably many occasions like a special birthday, your marriage, the birth of a child, your trip to Italy, your first kiss, your best friend, meeting Meryl Streep... (Hmm, that's on my bucket list)... that you wish to write about it. The following fun exercise will help you zoom in on what your favourite stories are.

Creating a Mind Map of Special Moments in Time

Supplies: A large piece of paper and a bunch of different coloured sharpies

In the centre of a large blank piece of paper or Bristol board, draw a circle and write the words: Special Moments in Time. Use the guidelines in the previous chapter for creating a mind map and make one for the special moments you have had throughout your life. Put the title in the centre circle and follow the instructions in Chapter 7. Add lots of spokes for the times in your life that were fun, exciting, honouring, and celebratory. Add your own adjectives of what makes these times special for you.

From each of your special events you have named, add more spokes with a few words to tweak your memory when you are ready to write about it. Say it was a significant move to a new house that made your heart sing. The spokes under that title (Significant Move) might say, 18 Maxwell Lane—Laura (perhaps she's a friend who was moving in with you or helped you pack up the boxes).

Once your mind map is complete, you can always add to it later as more special moments in time come to mind. The following guided meditation will help bring in the details of the particulars of each story. Use the same meditation for each.

Special Moments in Time

 Meditation and Writing Exercise

You may want to read and record this so that you can simply listen with your eyes closed. Or conversely, simply move into a relaxed state as instructed below.

Focus on your breath. Each breath brings you into a deeper state of relaxation, a sense of peace within.

Be aware of your thoughts and let them easily pass by without judgment and gently bring your focus back to your breath. Your breath is now moving to any area of your body that may feel tense. As you exhale, you release the tension and are feeling more and more calm, centred, and peaceful.

And now, in this relaxed state, allow one of the events you listed on your mind map to come into your consciousness. Be with that time now. Bring in the details. Do you remember the year or the season? What are you doing? What time of day or night is it? Who is with you? Is this something you were planning for quite some time or was it a complete surprise that delighted you then and delights you now as you remember it?

Consider everything you remember about this celebration, travel experience, et cetera, including the names of people who were with you (you can change the names later if you wish to publish). Think about the people you are going to delight as you recall these special events.

Now gently open your eyes and come back to this room, grab your journal and pen or go to your computer, have a glass of water nearby, and begin writing. Start with the name of the event, for example, "My thirteenth birthday surprise party." Start writing and enjoy.

After you choose your first story to write, continue to write the others you placed on your mind map as well as any events in this category that come to you. Write the stories in the order that you are inspired to write them. In other words, if you feel awesome about a particular story but you originally planned to write a different one that doesn't hold that much juice at the moment—go with the one that does. That's where you will have the most fun and the most flow.

When you are done writing these celebratory and feel-good stories, I hope you feel wonderful. You can decide whether you want to share them with your family and friends or publish them as a collection of stories that are a beautiful part of your history. Everyone loves feel-good stories. You never know whose heart you will open and whose day you will enhance by your sharing your special moments in time.

Now, ask yourself if you feel complete. As we know, life is not just a fiesta of feel-good times. Your life will contain challenging times as well. Times of heartbreak and loss. It's inevitable. The next step is an opportunity to write those stories that may still be up for healing. You know whether it is a sense of wanting to avoid going back and remembering situations that were painful that you don't want to look at, or whether you have, in fact, done a huge amount of healing already, and you simply are in a place now to move forward. That's beautiful and congratulations.

At this juncture, you can also look back at these feel-good stories and see what you have learned from them. Perhaps there were skills you acquired in your youth that put you in good stead throughout your life. For instance, remembering how, in order to get the accreditations you needed to graduate college, you worked part time. You were also looking after an ill family member which may inspire you to remember your resilience and what is possible when you set an intention and put your heart and mind to it. Sometimes, we just do things but haven't owned what it took to get us to there. Now is your time to acknowledge strengths and other qualities you have that you have taken for granted. This is your pat on the back time.

You can also look at what you wrote earlier about some of the things you loved to do when you were younger and allow them to motivate you on your next adventures moving forward. Perhaps your feel-good accomplishments and stories will become a one woman or man show or simply a joy to read to your children and grandchildren as time continues. Whatever you choose, you can be proud to have written them.

As well, if at some time down the road, stories from your past begin to surface and niggle at you to take an honest look at them in the eye, I have your back.

In the next chapter I will teach you how to navigate through past stories that carry pain with a beautiful opportunity to look at them, without blame, shame, regret, or remorse and put them behind you once and for all.

Chapter 9

How Deep Do I Dive (Part B)?
Putting the Past Behind Me Now

Step 6

I n this chapter, please allow me to lovingly take your hand and assist you in steering the rudders of your boat. We will move away from the rapids that still cause you pain in order to release the past and move toward the liberation you so strongly desire. It's understandable that you may have feelings of trepidation to go back in memory and recount the hardships that you faced, fearing you may drown in the sorrow such memories could evoke. I promise, if you follow my lead, you will not. Instead, you, as the adult who has survived all the events of your life, will capitalize on the strengths that got you through them. Here you will call in the troops of your inner resources, surrendering to the light of your higher wisdom, knowing on that level that the net will appear, and you will be strengthened by the courageous journey you have chosen to forge.

These are the stories that have made up your life written from a place of authenticity. This doesn't mean you don't feel afraid. It means that sometimes you really are, but are choosing a path that you know in the quiet of your centre, will help you lay your burdens down, knowing the truth shall set you free. Having taken these steps myself, I am confident of their ability to bring relief and release and once again, it is my joy and privilege to be your guide.

I invite you to begin by trusting in a Higher Plan. Acknowledge your feelings; love the parts of you that hurt at situations that occurred, leaving you weakened and sad; and then choose to stay on the side of what is working, and in fact, what's awesome.

Some people make complaining a habit and overlook the good in their lives. If you relate to that, you are about to turn the compass around and begin to see out of a new lens that shows you heaven on earth. Heaven is not a destination you go to after you die. It is a state of consciousness right here on our beautiful planet and you can access it right now. You can experience this with every breath of gratitude you breathe because you are alive and new, healthy choices are still available to you. When you choose to forge ahead upon the upper highway of Life, you will write your memoir with newfound courage and strength you didn't have when whatever circumstance befell you leaving you disempowered and afraid.

Are you ready to navigate the terrain that will bring you to brand-new beautiful vistas offering new opportunities for joy and happiness in your life? I am so excited to bring you to this choice point so that your book will reflect the truth of who you are: a beautiful child of God, ready to have life reflect your loveliness back to you at every turn.

This is a poem I wrote many years ago when I was hurting and angry and then remembered I was not alone. Neither are you. We are part of an omnipotent benevolent energy that wants the best for us at all times.

Ode to God

Just when I was losing hope
You came
Just when I was questioning my decisions
You came
Just when I was about to renege, there you were
And once again, I am being carried.
How do you do this?
How is it you see me at these moments of desperation?
And how do you know exactly what I want and then give it to me?
Of course, you don't always, now do you?
Although there would be those who would question that.
They would say, now, really, Junie, if it's happening, then you must have asked for it
On some level
And I want to punch them
Even though I'm not one for punching people
It occurs to me that it would feel good.
I would not only release my frustration; I would show them.
Now wouldn't I?

But I didn't need to.

I've never needed to.

You show up just in time.

I should have known.

Besides, if the truth be told, they do not judge me,

Simply hold up the mirror

It was hard to see anything when I looked into it

Because of all the cracks.

But that's where the light comes in, doesn't it

And that's where you greeted me. Again.

Once Again.

Mind Map

As with Chapter 8, Part A, you will do a mind map. Gather your supplies and in the centre of the large piece of paper write, "My Healing Stories."

For each of the spokes, give a title to the story that you wish to heal. Stories of events that perhaps came in as lambs but left as lions, leaving you bewildered by what happened. The stories that hurt you, left you heartbroken, bereft, uncertain, afraid, confused, grief stricken. Whatever the stories were that stole your life energy from you, your writing of them from a witness state will allow you to call your power back.

When you are ready to write your stories, I would like to remind you to not embody them. Instead, simply observe what happened from a safe distance as though you are watching it on a movie screen.

As a witness to what you see, you are also in the driver's seat. When you have had enough, walk away. Go outside for fresh air. Return to your gratitude journal and read what's in there to remind yourself about all the good stuff that's going on in your life today.

If you are used to a life of drama, it may be tempting to be seduced into remembering a particular betrayal or something else and want to talk about it with your friends. Do not.

Remember, whatever we focus on expands. Instead, focus on the way the sun is casting shadows on your window sill and your neighbour's cat, who's meowing at your door because you love to feed her. Choose to be fully in the moment

This is not a race; it is a process, and if you go too fast, you could retraumatize yourself. Ask yourself an honest question: "Am I ready to move deeper into this story at this time?"

If you are planning on recounting a time that you feel in your heart could retraumatize you, this would not be the time to go through this by yourself. Do you have a therapist you trust to do these processes with you? Often it is in the reading back of our stories with an unconditional loving witness present that helps us release the pain of the past. And remember, you have survived whatever occurred so you can choose for it not to hurt you anymore. Set that intention, but only you have that answer as to whether you should enter this past story alone at this time.

In my individual and group memoir-writing programs, I hold a safe space for healing to take place. As you read through these instructions, move slowly and gently and know what would be right for you. Then choose what will be in your highest interest at this time.

If you know you are ready to go beyond your comfort zone and dive into the story—that is calling to you the most—with an intention let go of the pain and learn what the inherent gifts and lessons are that story has come to teach you, gather your resilience tool box and keep it handy while writing the rest of the stories that you are wishing to heal.

For each of these stories, begin with the Invocation that I set out in Chapter Seven.

I shall repeat it here for you for easy access.

Invocation—Opening to the Gifts

As I prepare to write the following life story, I let go and let God. I am open and willing to receive the highest truth with respect to all that has happened to me. I acknowledge and accept that the people and circumstances in my life were brought to me for my learning, healing, and growth.

I am open to the gifts that the people and circumstances in this story offered me. I receive these gifts easily, graciously and with gratitude. I am letting go of any negative thinking that would cause me to deny the blessings that this life story offers. As I write my truth, I open to receive complete healing.

I take ownership and responsibility for the choices I have made. I love and forgive myself for any choices that hurt me and/or others. I am also ready and willing to forgive those who I perceive hurt me in any way. I am willing to see the innocence in myself and in them. I take a deep breath in and let go of any fear or tension I may be carrying.

I open to Universal grace and intelligence, helping to restore any imbalances for my highest good. Through the writing and remembering of this story and appreciation for the inherent gifts that were offered, I open to returning to a state of deep peace, health, and joy. I remember that everything I have experienced is for my soul's growth and evolution. I breathe in light and love. I give thanks as I begin to write and remember [name your story; e.g., "The Story of My First Husband, Fred"].

 ### Time to Write: [Name Your Healing Story and Write Where You Are]

In this chapter I will share a very personal story I wrote that only became public (in the form of a blog post) when Robin Williams took his life. It was the first time I revealed publicly my own attempts to take my life. I wasn't ready to tell that part of my history before then.

As stated earlier, I maintain that if we choose to write traumatic stories and include them in our memoir, we should do it when we feel safe and steady on our feet. We have a right to our privacy until we become clear it's time to share certain stories out loud.

I know from having lived on both sides of the couch—as patient and therapist—that post-traumatic stress syndrome can occur if we leap to tell our stories, especially when we are vulnerable and with people who do not support us and before we are grounded, balanced, and in harmony with the past.

I do not know your life history, but I can bet you have certain stories that have presented the greatest challenges for you. They made you work the hardest to overcome the pain left in their wake. It is these stories that you have triumphed over that offer you the greatest gifts. Perhaps it's the one that when you are ready to write it, the telling of that story will help countless others who need to hear your words. Words that reveal the healing balm that will help them in the ways it has helped you.

Here is my story that spilled out of me at the exact right time and indeed became a catalyst and healing balm for myself first and then for many of my clients and writing students. As we are part of one humanity, suicide affects us all. It is not an easy subject to talk about and few ever do. If this applies to you, I hope that my story will help you to feel less alone and is a stepping stone in helping you to release any pain still associated with Robin William's death by suicide or that of a loved one.

I also want you to know that if you have attempted to take your life, I extend my hand and my heart to you. Please know it is not your fault. I know that kind of unrelenting mental torture that plagues you into believing that your life is hopeless and things will never change. I urge you, if you are feeling this way now, I urge you to reach out to a true friend, a Help Line, a mental health service in your area. Your life can absolutely change for the better even though it feels absolutely impossible right now. I am sending you my love, strength and courage. If you are on the other side of an attempt, know that you are here for a reason. It's true. There's a meaningful, joyful life ahead awaiting you. I am so happy you are writing down your life stories. Make sure you write about this experience as it is probably one of the most significant realities in your life. What can be more crucial than life and death. I wish you a long, healthy, creative and blessed life. You can see the relationship between creativity and mental health here: https://junieswadron.com/mental-health/ It is about a vision I hold – called ACHA Academy for Creative and Healing Arts (an integrated centre for people with mental health challenges and the people who love them).

Here is my story that came gushing out of me like an avalanche at the news of Robin William's death.

Death by Suicide: There but for the Grace of God, Go I

I can't imagine one person who has heard about Robin Williams's death who hasn't been shocked and devastated.

I live with bipolar illness. I was diagnosed when I was twenty years old. I "came out" when I was fifty years old. It was too freakin' scary to do it before then. It was terrifying even then. After all, I had a private psychotherapy practice, worked as a mental health worker in a group home, and gave educational talks in corporations about mental health in the workplace sponsored by the Canadian Mental Health Association. How could I "come out of the closet" and expect my career to survive. How could *I* expect to survive?

I had just come out of a hospital after another clinical depression. The phones were ringing. People were wanting to come to my new workshops. I couldn't do it. I couldn't lie any more. I couldn't go back to pretending all was well with me when I had spent the last month in a psych ward.

Instead I wrote Madness, Masks and Miracles, a play about the dark night of the soul that everyone on earth experiences at least once in life. I wrote about the masks we wear to disguise the pain. Who would ever have known of the unspeakable burden that Robin Williams was carrying? Many of us have learned to have a public facade that can fool the masses. And finally, my play was about the miracles that allow us to take off our masks and be who we really are.

I am one of the lucky ones. I count my blessings. I have had numerous suicide attempts. I can't describe to you or anyone what I have come to call "the torture chamber of the mind." Thank God, for the past eight years I have been well. Really well.

I've had my moments of unrest, sadness, being overwhelmed. I have never even come close to having suicidal thoughts. I don't believe I ever will again. The last attempt led me to a near-death experience, and I woke up in a state of grace and have never looked back.

I am inspired right now to tell this story. A story I have never told in public. The people close to me know it. I have always been too ashamed to tell it. Me—the one who "came out of the closet" all those years ago standing on stage at the Vancouver Conference Centre in front of four hundred doctors and mental health workers at the International World Assembly for Mental Health, a convention that happened to be in Vancouver when we just started staging the play.

They heard of us. They asked us to perform it for them. It was the worst experience I have ever encountered. It was also the best experience, as it allowed me to speak my truth—in spite of the terror of being criticized, ostracized, marginalized, and hospitalized one more time.

Then just eight years ago, in 2009, which also feels like light years ago—I "woke up" in what I described earlier as a state of grace. But the story that preceded it was not pretty. Few people know about it. Today, I came to the computer intending to do something else. Instead my fingers are flying off the keyboard telling this story—one I was always too ashamed to tell.

Bipolar illness, and every other mental illness, has many shapes and sizes. It is not a cookie-cutter disease as some people may think. "Oh, look, she's really depressed. Oh look, she's wildly out of control." There are so many layers. Oh, so many. And the sufferer of these illnesses and their family, friends, and caregivers suffer right along with them.

When I was a young girl, and up until recently, no one spoke about their mental illness, especially not in public. The stigma and shame was so unbearably powerful that no one dared. Hey, I didn't dare until I was fifty.

Today, and for several years now, public figures are talking freely about their diagnoses, their pain and suffering. Mental illness is talked about in the media more now than ever—at least here in North America. Still, there is a long way to go. And it is people who do speak out that make it safe for others to do the same.

I have been speaking out for a long time now. It doesn't mean I am comfortable with it. The fear of being judged is always there. Even a couple of weeks ago, I posted something on Facebook that referred to my mental health challenges. I got absolutely no response. A few days earlier I wrote a funny story about getting married, and I got upwards of eighty likes and comments. Yet there were no comments when I mentioned my illness. I felt judged and ashamed and removed it from Facebook.

And here I am again coming out even deeper. Admitting my suicide attempts. Am I crazy to do this? Apparently, I am crazy. Or am I not crazy? Am I wise or am I just a person who knows only too well the dangers of secrets, denial, self-loathing, and hiding in shame? Whatever I may be, all I know is that my fingers are flying off the keyboard, and I know I am not manic. I am being propelled by an inner voice, an energy that says, "There is nothing to hide, Junie. You didn't do anything wrong." Funny how often I still think that.

In 2009 I was raced by ambulance to the Royal Jubilee Hospital in Victoria with hardly a pulse. I had swallowed over one hundred prescription pills; dozens were sleeping pills. I did not intend to come back. I needed to get out of what I have called "the torture chamber of my mind," a relentless diatribe in my brain, obsessive, cruel, heart-crushing thoughts of guilt and suicidal ideation—and a body riddled with anxiety and a foreboding that never went away. Month after month after month, after month, and I couldn't bear it any longer.

I swallowed one hundred pills. It was terrifying. I did not want to die. I love life—as strange as that may seem. I just wanted out of this body, this mind, this pain that wouldn't stop—something that no one could see because I have honed the disguise so well. I could even go to work. I could even hear and respond to people in a way that no one would have guessed I was suffering. But I knew, and I knew I could not hide it any longer.

I wrote letters to the people I loved, gulping down tears, and then emptied out dozens of vials filled with prescription drugs and swallowed them all. I was sobbing so loud I was sure neighbours could hear me, but I couldn't stop. I apologized to God and to every family member, to the friends who loved me, to the clients who depended on me, to my pets, to the world. And I did it anyway. Once again, as in earlier attempts, I called no one. Not a family member, a friend or an emergency line. I just wanted out because I didn't believe anyone could help me. I had lost every ounce of hope that I would ever be able to be well again.

A neighbour who knew I was depressed and had my keys to feed my budgie birds when I went away checked in on me. I was told she found me on the floor in the kitchen where I swallowed the pills. She called the ambulance; they raced me to the hospital, but I was already in a coma that lingered for three days and nights. Then, miraculously, on the fourth day, I opened my eyes and talked. I felt better than I could ever remember. The doctors were stunned. Not only were they convinced I would not survive, but they were certain if I did, I would have irreparable brain and organ damage. I had neither. Physically, I was well. Mentally, I was in what I can only call "a state of grace."

They removed all the tubes and wires from my body and transferred me to Eric Martin Pavilion, the psychiatric hospital in the city. To me, it was an ashram.

No, I did not think I was Jesus, going from person to person blessing everyone. I simply sat silently observing the dozens of men and women in that big room, all beautiful souls, suffering, lost and in turmoil—just like I had been before I "woke up." I had nothing but compassion for them as well as for the staff. I could see their frustration and their own suffering and how they were trying so hard to do their best. During this time of observation, I felt grounded, centred, and at peace in a way I never had before known.

Two days after coming out of coma, I asked a friend of mine to bring me my computer. I knew it was time to write my book. How was that possible? For the past six months or longer I had not even been able to string a sentence together. Even writing a short email to confirm a meeting, for example, caused unbearable anxiety, let alone writing in my journal. And for me, usually it is writing that helps the best to bring me solace. And I've been teaching this for about twenty years. Before my suicide attempt that was virtually impossible. There were no words.

Something inside of me said, "You must have your computer." It was brought to me and within nine months, my book *Re-Write Your Life: A Transformational Guide to Writing and Healing the Stories of Your Life* was completed and published.

From not being able to write anything, I found words of wisdom flowing out of me with deep passion, and I was loving every moment of it. Why? Because I knew, only too well, as both clinician and patient, that it is only in rewriting our painful stories that we find peace. That hanging on to the past—in shame, guilt, blame, resentments, grief, sorrow, and unforgiveness—will never lead to happiness. It only keeps us stuck. Paralyzed. Grandiose. Depressed. Needing to be right—at any cost. It keeps us anywhere but in our hearts.

I knew beyond any doubt—having almost died—that life is precious, oh, so precious. And it is not a dress rehearsal. It's real. The years go by. We grow older. And we will die one day, and, my God, if I could help even one person find a way to live life in peace and in joy and to let go of the past and celebrate their life journey instead, nothing was going to stop me. I was going to write and publish that book.

I knew this was the most important work I had done up until that time. I had rewritten many of my stories already. Now, from this blessed state, I wrote with an inner conviction of truth that would free not only me but also others who were drawn to its message.

I still live by it. Yet even now, in this moment, as I sit in front of this computer, the conviction of speaking my truth out loud is still there, but so is the fear of being judged. I'm not sure if that will ever go away. But how could I even think of that stopping me? I am alive. Robin Williams is not. Nor are countless millions of others across our planet who have ended their lives and possibly as many still who are on the brink as I write this.

How could I not speak up? How can we not? Together, as one human family, speak up and out, hold each other's hands, stop judging, and find our way back to our tender hearts.

Robin Williams, a brilliant, beautiful, courageous man who brought joy and laughter into the lives of millions of people is dead. Dead by suicide.

I happened to be at movie on Monday ironically held at Eric Martin—the mental hospital I was hospitalized in—where they play brilliant movies and the like. Monday night I was there to watch the documentary, *Of Two Minds*, which was riveting—a stunning depiction of several people living with bipolar illness. It was sad, funny in parts, and, oh, so very, real. But my friend, who I was saving a seat for, sat down and told me the news about Robin Williams. I had to leave the theatre and go to the bathroom because I started to cry. Once I was in the bathroom, in a lone stall, I allowed myself to sob. In the most sad and ironic way, it is in his death that I am given the courage to come out once again—to come out of the closet about my own attempted suicides.

I am hoping in doing so I will be able to let go of some of the guilt and shame that I attempted to take my life. I am doing my best to reach into my heart and offer myself compassion for the states of terror and hopelessness that drove me to want to do that. I needed to reassure myself that I didn't do anything to purposely cause pain and suffering to others. If I or anyone else who is at that critical place could make a rational choice to do it differently, to find a magical cure to be well again and not hurt themselves or the people who love them and they love too—oh, if only. If only.

Since the last attempt, I have been living in deep gratitude and deep humility. There isn't a day that goes by when I do not remember to thank God. Why me? Why was my life spared and not his? Not countless others. I don't know. I only know I am here. And I am here to make a difference in whatever ways I can.

And one of the ways, I sense, is in writing this book and sharing it out loud with you. And tomorrow and the day after that, it will hopefully be with words and deeds of kindness for whomever shows up on my path.

And that's what we can all do. We can't all be writers or social activists on the front lines. But we can offer gifts of kindness—first to ourselves, by nurturing ourselves into healthy minds and bodies and spreading the kindness to every living being we meet.

Even though years have passed since I was shaken to my core at Robin William's death and my need to come out of hiding about my own suicide attempts, it still feels vulnerable and raw to write about it here in this book even though I have come so much further. That's how hard it is sometimes to let go of old tapes carrying the pain and shame of being judged.

Dear reader, please, as you embark on writing your own memoir including stories that are still excruciating to write, do not write them with the intention of publication. Write them with the intention of healing. Write them for your own inner catharsis because writing has magic powers, and then, if need be, read and process what you have written with a therapist or someone else you trust to safely hold a loving space for you, someone who will not judge, just be a loving witness to your tender heart.

Then, one day when a situation arises that reminds you of this same circumstance—something that would normally trigger you and you find, instead, that you hardly notice it—you can safely say, you have put it to bed. You can look at yourself square in the eyes in the mirror and say, "Hey, beautiful, you did it. It's over." Or conversely, you still feel sadness but it no longer carries the weight it did. If, like me when Robin Williams died, you are catapulted to your computer to pound out the avalanche of feelings that accompany your pain, know you are ready to release the anguish you have been carrying. That which flowed from my pen on August 11, 2014, reminding me of my own suicide attempts and causing me to question how I survived—and more, how I have thrived—once again brought me to my knees in unwavering gratitude. Today, only five years later—almost to the day—I acknowledge once again what I stated earlier—we can't ever know why unsuspecting sorrow crosses our path or the paths of our brethren, we can only acknowledge that Life has its own mysterious reasons. And knowing that, it's best we allow ourselves all the feelings that are there to be expressed—not to deny them or rail against that which has already happened, but to summon the love that still prevails and always will, and move ever forwards towards the season where the frozen waters begin to flow again in order to live Robin Williams's famous words, "Spring is nature's way of saying, 'Let's party.'" I raise my glass to you, Mr. Williams, for your enormous heart and reminding us to party, to laugh, to celebrate. I hope you knew how loved you were and still are. May you rest in peace.

Chapter 10

The Brand New You: Take a Bow

Step 7

W ell, now. Look at you. Seriously, go take a look in the mirror. Put on your most spectacular smile and then turn up the music and dance.

Can you feel the different state you are in now?

Once you start valuing yourself, you can say, "Yes, of course, I do" and become motivated from a place of strength and service. That is what Step 7 is all about. Every new day that you can take steps in the direction of your goals in precisely the same way as you have while writing your memoir, you can rejoice. In fact, each time you do reinforces your newly attuned ear to hear the voice of your inner guidance moving you along the path of resurrection—of new meaning, confidence, and satisfaction.

It's so much fun to live life from inner motivation and inspiration than in the dangerous quicksand of never-ending to-do lists, carrying musts, have-to's, and guilt.

Do you carry the identity of the senior citizen without a plan, feeling used up, and unvalued with nothing to mark your retirement days with anymore? Or are you a person – perhaps a student, or an entrepreneur, stay at home mom or dad or something else that still questions, "Who am I to write my life stories? Not in the least!

Just who was that person who resided in your body? You took a stand and moved toward your dreams and you accomplished them. No longer will your ego have its way with you until you are either under the train or arrive at the terminal just in time to watch it leave the station.

Not this time. Now you are on that train carrying you to the destinations that please you. You can stand proud. Walk proud. Take a bow because you are on your way to sharing your story with your friends and family and perhaps are considering publication as you take stock of what you have learned and the gifts your life stories have taught you. Now it is you who are a mentor for those wanting to hop on that same train. You get to teach what you have learned and spread the wisdom that you now embody. That is when we all get to be teachers and students alike.

I generally start my classes with this question, "Who believes that when the student is ready, the teacher appears?" Usually everyone raises their hand. Then I ask them, "Who believes when the teacher's ready, the student appears?" And they are taken aback a bit because they didn't expect that.

That's what reflecting on your life stories will teach you—that everyone in your life has been a student or a teacher or an earth angel sent to you for your growth and evolution. Those who read your particular stories could be currently struggling just like you were during one of the hardest challenges in your life and your words will motivate them into becoming the champion of their lives and because of it, they too one day will pass the baton.

Many years ago, during one of my first writing workshops, I gave the writing prompt, "Waiting." One of the men in the group wrote about waiting to die and a suicide pact he and his friend made during a night of partying with too many glasses of wine, beer, and scotch. When he woke up after passing out, he noticed his friend lying dead beside him with a gun next to his body.

It was the first time Chris shared this story ever, with anyone. Obviously, I didn't race to give the next writing exercise. Instead all of us held him as he sobbed and wailed.

About ten years ago, I received a book in the mail entitled From Chris to Christian. It was written by this same person, my former student. A letter was tucked inside the front cover of his book. In it he stated he will never forget the night that story spilled out of him and of being held by myself and the group. He said it was the beginning of his healing journey and that I can read many of the stories now written in a book he is proud of. He said writing his memoir helped him recover. Clarity rose up from murky waters allowing him to make new choices and turn his life around. He is now a happily married man with family he adores and is the minister in a small Ontario town. His note ended with, "Thank you, Junie for setting me on this path of writing and healing. I will always be eternally grateful." We were there for Chris on that pivotal night—a catalyst in his recovery. Writing his memoir was a big step along his healing journey. An empowering step that will now be the inspiration for readers far and wide.

 ### *Writing Exercise: Awesome Things I Have Done and Am Proud Of*

This is a free-flow, writing exercise to state the awesome things you have done in your life. Let your healthy ego have its day in the sun by giving it (you) a standing ovation. After all, you have an amazing future to look forward to as an author leaving a legacy of triumph and paving the way for countless others to have a life of hope, meaning, recovery, and joy.

By now, you know the drill. Have your glass of water ready and leave yourself at least one hour to write undisturbed. This time, after your writing, ask your little child inside what she or he would like to do and go do it.

About now, mine would like an ice cream cone, but it's only 9:00 in the morning.

Chapter 11

Sacred Stories, Celebrating
Your Life Journey Book Launch

Step 8

W ell done! You have made your dream, the one that kept coming back, to write your memoir or life stories come true! Congratulations!

Of course, once it has been written, and you choose to publish it, there are steps you need to take. Those steps are not outlined in this book which specifically teaches you how to write your stories. However, I can tell you that the publishing industry has changed in significant ways. You now have a choice as to whether you wish to self-publish your book or go with a traditional publisher; there is a great deal to learn, starting with knowing what both entail. Once you have done your due diligence, chosen your publishing method, and have your book in your hand you will get to show it off at your book launch. Sweet, right! Yes, you can indeed be proud. I know what that's like, and it is truly exhilarating. I am so excited for you.

Step 8, the final step is to prepare you for your book launch, I will take you on a guided visualization in respect and reverence for all the work you lovingly put into the process of writing your memoir. You followed the steps, wrote the stories you have lived—often moving, poignant, ironic, or humorous—the ones that shaped your life in significant ways, making you who you are.

And now you are ready to hold the event that you have been dreaming of—standing on a stage as an author. For each person it will be different. Your stage could be a living room with your family and close friends. It could be a large hall with hundreds of people coming to celebrate you while you read from selected chapters and share from your heart what lessons life has taught you.

In preparation for this guided meditation, you may want to record it so that you can simply sit back and listen. Or if not, simply begin by becoming conscious of your breath. Breathe in deeply, relax and let go. And feel the relaxation come with every breath. Exhale any tension you are feeling in your body and inhale joy, peace, and tranquillity Feel yourself let go, feeling free, happy, and relaxed.

Imagine yourself now at your book launch. Where are you? Is it someone's living room or perhaps your own home surrounded by family and close friends as you share stories from your life, some they have never heard. Picture them intrigued, spellbound and delighted to know you in this new way.

Or perhaps you are you in an auditorium filled with your favourite people as well as many you've never seen before. Everyone is there to celebrate you and your brand-new book.

Who do you see? What are you wearing? What time of day is it? Bring in all the details. What stories have you decided to read from your book? What stories are you intending to tell as a way of sharing your experience in writing the book, the lessons you learned that you are now ready to impart?

See everyone smiling at you, loving your words and your inspiration, joining you in your accomplishment, celebrating your life journey and proud to be there, ready to tell their friends about you and your book. You are so excited. Are you looking forward to more presentations to offer the wisdom you have gleaned over your lifetime?

This is your dream and you get to go first class. You are creating your future as you passionately imagine your book launch. There you are centre stage at the front of the room holding your book, embracing the excitement you feel in your body. If you are in a large auditorium, feel the excited buzz in the room. See yourself standing proud, feeling amazing, relaxed, joyous and on top of the world. This is your most confident, awesome self. Imagine the enthusiastic applause as you entertain and enlighten your guests with your stories. At the end of the evening, see a line-up of people purchasing your book. You are autographing it for them while they are praising you for your work and letting you know what an inspiration you are.

Imagine being back home afterward, basking in the glory of your accomplishment. You did it. You can stand proud.

Now, take another deep breath and in your own time, gently breathe yourself back into this moment and get ready to write about your experience.

 ### *Journal Writing Exercise: My Book Launch*

In this writing exercise, which is to be done in your journal, write in first person, present tense, all about your book launch, the way you just imagined it. Write in all the details. Get excited about it. Feel the excitement in every bone in your body. Know that your book launch is truly a feat you can look forward to. You stand among other authors now and your life will never look the same again.

Chapter 12

Obstacles

As much as I would love to know that the previous chapter is the truth for you, that you have indeed written your life stories having used the processes in this book and are standing tall, holding book launches, and sharing your wealth of information and stories that have moved you from sadness to celebration, this may not be your current reality.

Instead, have your old self-sabotaging programs taken over the show? Instead of rejoicing, are you ruminating on the plans that never took hold and the ten thousand heartbreaks you have lived?

Is this just another one of those times you have you read a book, seen a movie, taken a workshop, or gone on a personal growth retreat determined to follow through on something you truly wanted but then, within a few weeks, you were back to the same old, self-defeating patterns? You let the opportunity slip from your fingertips. Please do not waste your time beating yourself up. It is time consuming, counterproductive and won't get you ultimately where you want to go. I know what will though. And so do you. Of course you do and I'm still beside you as your guide. I know what it feels like to be stuck. I also know how it feels when I choose to get unstuck. It is bliss! I want you to look at yourself square in the face and make a new choice. One that will liberate you and illuminate your new path. The one you chose when you picked up this book. Your Life Matters. You know that at your core. And I know it for you.

Let me tell you again, life is not a dress rehearsal. It's the real deal, and we only get to live it once. Whatever fears you carried throughout your life, are they still there? Do they linger in the corners, or crawl out unbidden in the middle of the night?

Those patterns you have are pretty dug in and unless you are willing to go the distance, all the way, no more halfway measures, you can expect the same thing to happen this time too.

With all good intentions, have you allowed the demands on your life—the needs of aging parents, your children, your partner or some other circumstance to take front and centre stage? There's an adage: no matter how awful, there's no place like home. It's what's familiar. It's easier than expecting much more of ourselves. Or is it? Actually, it clearly is not, unless you are basking in your disappointment. There's always some secondary gain. Without judgement, you can ask yourself what you have to gain any more by staying stuck. What young part of you is still needing love and attention that you can now give her or him?

This is where the rubber meets the road. If you want to achieve your dreams to write your memoir but it's just not coming together, working with a mentor will support you to ensure the results you are looking for. Just like a rocket ship has boosters to transcend the gravitational pull that wants to pull it back to earth, we need support structures in place to keep us moving forward.

Although moving beyond the past can be truly challenging, what will it cost you to stay where you are? To not write your memoir, to not grow because of it, to not have all the dreams you associated with writing your life stories come true?

Were you hoping to offer others what you have come to know through some of the biggest hurdles you faced? Don't you think that not doing it would be a travesty? Where would humanity be if everyone who has achieved wisdom through their life experience lacked the confidence to share it with others? Where would you be? No further than you are now, I'm afraid. This doesn't have to be your fate.

I extend my hand to you so that you are not isolated and alone. You will come to appreciate that at the core of your being is a centre of beauty, wisdom, love, and joy which you can learn to access at any time in order to receive your own inner guidance. The result will be greater peace and ease in your life—and confidence—in spades. You will notice how your life begins to flow in harmonious ways. Synchronistic and serendipitous events start to become a natural part of your daily living. This is what happens when we change our perceptions, take charge of our lives and recognize that we're not a victim of circumstance.

You are a soul who came here with your own unique dreams, desires, creativity, and abilities. And no matter how it has been so far in your life, no matter where you are on the continuum of fear to love, or on the continuum of writing your memoir—some stories written, or perhaps none or nearing the end, you are now in a new choice point to take action—releasing your old comfort zone of inertia to move into the light of all who you are becoming.

I recognize that putting your voice out into the world in the form of a published work is a big deal. Even when it's just for the individuals closest to you, it's a big deal. It's a reflection of you–your imagination, thoughts, opinions, and often your tender heart. If you are not used to being "out there," it can be terrifying. I know first-hand that feeling of terror. I also know first-hand how it feels to hold my book in my hands, to have surpassed that paralyzing road block. And I know the relief and feelings of safety and empowerment when working with a coach who gets me, guides me and keeps me on task. You can know that, too. You can experience a new sense of aliveness along with the curiosity of a child. The darkened shadows of the past can be part of your newfound strength. They have brought you to this new life with a bedrock foundation of faith, courage, resilience, and freedom.

As you read these words, allow yourself to feel into the aliveness that your life will bring you when you take whatever steps are necessary to fulfil this dream. Doing this, you choose the high road. As you allow me to take your hand beyond the pages of this book, the dream that has been calling your name time and time again will come harmoniously to fruition.

I have watched people over my career of close to thirty years whose self-sabotaging behaviours continued running the show and never allowed them to reach their dreams. I have seen so many more surpass their dreams to live a life, often beyond what they could have ever imagined.

This is your life. This is the real show. The only show. Yes, this is it. Do not live one more day stopping yourself from living a life you love. You will not get this day back ever again.

No matter what dire things have happened in the past, the past is over unless you keep it alive by the beliefs you store inside of you.

Haven't you built enough fortresses to dull the pain? Do you realize those walls are also keeping out the love you deserve? If you have truly had enough, let the buck stop here. Say YES to reclaiming your life. Be among the thousands of students who have leaned in and been guided personally by myself, a woman who has done just that. I surpassed my fears and came to the place where I knew my life was sacred and that I matter and my stories were worth telling. Dear reader, your life matters! And I know your stories are so worthwhile. I intend to honour you every step of the way as you go forth to write your memoir. You can return to the beginning of the book with new vigour and promise as all the steps are here to help you write a sensational memoir. Or simply drop me a line at junie@ junieswadron.com and we'll work it out together, beyond these pages if you prefer.

I reinforce the teachings on these pages that help heal your frightened inner child while coming to know your adult gifts, strengths, and capabilities. You will learn how to keep your heart open. How to re-parent yourself with love, tenderness, kindness, and compassion and touch the truth within you where your wisdom, beauty, love, and truth reside. When you tap into this creative life-force energy, you raise your vibration and your life unfolds in new and wondrous ways.

Chapter 13

A Stunning Accomplishment

C ongratulations! You have written your book in the form of a memoir or perhaps as a series of meaningful life stories. What a stunning accomplishment. I truly acknowledge you for your willingness to go back into your past, to visit old circumstances and events—pleasant and unpleasant—and to give yourself the gift of honouring your life.

It is through this journey of self-reflection that you come to see the full meaning of your life and the growth that you have achieved over the years. You can look at all the people who have brought you love, comfort, and encouragement. And you can also see with increased clarity all the people who entered your life presenting challenges and thus giving you an opportunity to heal your heart and move forwards.

You walked consciously into the past, back into old pain to make sense of it with an intention to let in the light—to heal and move forward. Doing this you can expect that your life will now reflect all the effort you put in as you watch it unfold with joy, grace and ease.

Your job is to live in today much more than in the hurtful stories of the past. It is clear that each of these stories have come to teach you something important about your life. Embrace that opportunity and open to the gifts that will reveal themselves to you. Stay steadfast in your gratitude practices and in knowing the truth of who you are.

In earlier exercises where you imagined holding and loving your inner child who experienced so much trauma, know that as you approach these stories, you are setting up the conditions for full transformation. Writing your stories with the intention to heal allowed you to integrate the child self with your adult self, and you will find that you will show up differently in the world. The processes in *Your Life Matters*, has been helping you to call your spirit back and your life energy will return to you in ways you may not have anticipated.

The book you thought you might write will take on a whole new look—because a whole new you has written it. It will be an inspired achievement—written from the you who knows her or his worth. As well, all the adventures you have had in your life—your travels, volunteer work, career, intimate relationships, friendships, children—all that you wish to write about will be coming from an enlightened awareness instead of a simple recounting of facts.

Be ready for this transformation because that is what you can expect the more you honour who you are. I recommend you continue to journal as a sacred tool to call forth the divine within you. Our pens magically access parts of us that our brains simply cannot find.

Did you notice how writing your stories was a catalyst for newfound hope and freedom—that as you asked inside for guidance, you became a conduit for Universal intelligence to flow through you revealing new insights and memories and becoming your elixir for healing and understanding.

You discovered what it feels like to write yourself home where your truth awaited you—where your authentic voice on the page has become the voice you are now putting out to the world. No more hiding behind walls of self-imprisonment called fear. Your willingness to go naked and be vulnerable in order to claim back your voice moved you on a path of resurrection where you were able to truly bring about closure to lifelong anger, regrets, resentments, and pain.

By following the processes in this book, applying the healing power of intention, courage, and commitment, you made your dream come true. Truly, what a stunning accomplishment!

Over time, you will find that those things that have scared you will stop scaring as you come to believe in yourself more and more. Your shyness gets replaced with a willing curiosity to try new things and see how they go. You will be able to say no and mean it and say yes and mean it and know when both are true. And you will begin to see your life as an elder as one of the most important times of all. You will become the mentors you have been watching and hoping you could be like. Or you are at a place where you value yourself more than ever before no matter what your age. You are the person you've been searching for all along.

Do you remember the answers you wrote to the four questions near the beginning of the book, regarding your memoir of what you wanted, needed, feared, and hoped for? As you look back now, how would you answer them today?

It is my desire that you received what you wanted and needed in order to accomplish this feat. I pray that your fears have been dispelled and that you have learned through the processes of mind mapping to love your inner child and celebrate all of who you are. It is also my deepest wish for you that you have come to indeed know you are worthy and that your life and all you have lived truly matters.

And now that you have accomplished this dream, what is it you hope for? As we climb one mountain and get to the summit, we often find there is another one we aspire to. That is life calling us again to fulfil new dreams for our personal evolution and growth. What are yours?

If your new dream is to share publicly that which you have learned, I encourage you to take all your newfound confidence and make it happen. Let the words in your newly written memoir be your voice in the world to guide those who need your advice. Being an author puts you in a category of being an authority of what you know, and you know that you know a great deal. You have indeed acquired a great deal of wisdom ready to be stated out loud using your book made up of your transformational stories, as your resource to offer others.

As we come to the conclusion, I wish to offer you this one last exercise to keep you motivated and moving forward.

Take time to reread the stories you have written. Not in a way you might before you give them over to an editor for publication. No, read them now as a way of looking back to acknowledge how far you have come and how rich your life has been. Acknowledge your strengths and how courageous you have been to move through some difficult times. As you do this, bless your life, all the experiences in it, and all the people who have walked this journey with you.

Looking at it now from twenty-twenty vision, are there other important lessons you have learned along the way? In what way can the wisdom you have gained from these life events assist you as you go into the future? What would you like to remember the next time you have a challenging experience?

 Journal Writing Exercise: What Matters Now Is...

In your journal, finish this sentence: What matters now is…

I love Julia Cameron's words "Our creativity is our gift from God. Doing our creativity is our gift back to God."

In other words, you have written your book; you stand as an authority of what you have learned. In fact, you are a master at it, and it is a beautiful thing to take up your place of honour in service to others. Your voice on stages where you can impart your learnings to people who are currently facing challenges that you learned to surpass, is your gift back to God. Your gift back to humanity.

Or perhaps you are not inspired to speak from a stage. Instead, in braving the pages in the way you have, healing your own life stories, you are offering a triumphant legacy that can replace familial stories of shame, blame, regret and sorrow with new opportunity for hope, growth, transformation, and resurrection. You are setting the stage for those who come after you to walk in footsteps fostered by kindness, courage, strength, and inspiration. Well done. You can indeed walk proud!

Appendix A

Meditation: The Gift of the Child

I invite you to close your eyes and follow your breath inward. Be with yourself right now. Be with your breath right now.

Let go of anything that takes you out of this moment, of this one precious moment.

Take a mindful breath in and breathe out a smile. And another. Be still. Allow the stillness to enfold you. Softly. Gently. Feel the ecstasy here. The undulating joy in the stillness of presence.

I am about to take you on a journey. A journey where you will have an opportunity to give the very most of yourself. Where you will give from the divine feminine of yourself. Even if you are a man, you will give from this place of nurturance. And you shall receive from this place too. The act of giving and receiving where there is love without limits is the purest form of grace that humans encounter.

Let the journey begin. Once again, it begins with breath. Conscious breath. You are in a room in a large, beautiful house. It is your house. It is bright. The walls are a soft hue of your favourite colours. The sun is streaming from the windows. The curtains are blowing slightly from a spring breeze. You can smell the lilacs infusing the living room from the lilac bush outside your window. The hallway from the living room leads to a bright open kitchen with floor-to-ceiling windows that open out to the patio garden. The flowers here are red and blue and pink and purple. There are roses and tulips. There are petunias and sunflowers. There are daffodils and daisies, and you step outside and feel the sun on your body. You feel the breeze caress your face. You have poured yourself a tall glass of cranberry and soda with a squeeze of lemon, which you put down on the table next to the chaise lounge where you are about to meditate.

You lie down on the lawn chair, adjust it so it is at the perfect height for you, and close your eyes. You hear the birds singing from the trees in your yard and the neighbours' yards. And that is all the sounds there are. There is nothing else but you and the songbirds, and you breathe deeply into the silence of your heart.

You then hear music, music that you have never heard before. It is like an angel choir. And now accompanying the music are words. Words cascading over you like milk and honey. You are being told that a very special gift is on its way to you. You will be very surprised. And you feel a sense of peace and also excited anticipation.

Then you wake up. What an interesting dream. You ask, Have I been dreaming? It was so real. You stretch, open your eyes. You reach for your cool drink and just then, the doorbell rings.

You aren't expecting anyone. In fact, you left a space for yourself this weekend to have no plans other than to nurture yourself. You let your friends and family know you would be away. You wonder if you should answer it. It wouldn't be surprising if it's your neighbour who saw your car in the driveway and just wants to come for a visit, a chat. She's lonely. How many times have you stopped what you were doing, offered her tea and your time, and neglected the tasks at hand? Perhaps you won't answer it. Not this time.

But even as you are thinking these thoughts, you are feeling compelled to answer the door. You walk around the path leading from the back garden into the front yard towards the front door. There's no one there. And then you see it.

There's a basket—a large basket. You walk up to it. Look in, and there's the most beautiful baby you have ever seen, looking up at you. And the baby smiles. As you look down at it, your whole body is filled with an emotion that you can't even describe. Tears begin to fall from your eyes. Chills run through every vein. You remember your dream—that you are about to receive a gift. Could this really be happening?

There is a note. All it says is, "This is your child. This child is here for you to love and nurture with all your heart."

You look through your veil of tears and begin to notice the similarities of this baby, this child, and in a moment's recognition, you know that the baby is you and you are the baby, and you are here to love and receive love in a way that you never have before.

You are overcome with love and sadness at the same time. Looking into the eyes of this child that is you, you see everything. You see the love and tenderness, the innocence, and purity—the true you. The one who was born free—free to speak, to dance, to cry, to take naps, to sing, to tell the truth, to be inventive, and to love nature and animals and life.

And you see and know only too well the other part of this baby, this child—the one who was so painfully wounded, that had its childhood innocence stolen when you learned from others that you had to be quiet or that what you said didn't matter, or that you weren't smart or talented, which broke your heart. You often felt isolated and alone, but you learned you couldn't speak your truth and you couldn't cry, so you learned to put on masks to hide your pain. Dreaming and creating and being magnificent was for other people.

In time your spontaneous, joyous, beautiful child that loves to sing and dance and write and play feels like an ancient dream that you can't quite touch anymore. Ahh, but you can. You look again at this baby, and you see its innocence and purity, and you reach down and pick this baby up, and you hold her or him in your arms, and nothing has ever felt this right before. Nothing. And you know the miracle that has been bestowed on you. And you declare in this very moment that you will honour this child with every beat of your heart. You look at her or him again, smile and say:

Welcome beautiful baby—precious child. Welcome to the world and welcome to my life. You can also listen to this being read by me on a beautiful phone App of meditations called, Insight Timer. Just type in my name.

Write-fully yours,

Junie

Appendix B

Breathing Possibilities

You can talk about yesterday or talk about tomorrow
You can talk about the falling dollar, talk about your sorrow
You can talk about chemicals and how they're poisoning the earth
You can talk about how bad it is and how it's getting worse
Or you can take this moment and softly close your eyes
Breathe a breath from deep within and do not compromise
Take another and then another and in the stillness feel
The wonder of this moment—can this too be real?
Stay within the silence and notice what you hear
Listen with your heart and watch your fears all disappear
For in this moment, a miracle is due
If you listen with your heart there will be a message just for you.

A child is being born right now; can you hear the sound of life

In a little church just down the way vows are being made as man and wife

Somewhere on a hilltop a traveller has found her way

And the dew upon the morning grass has welcomed a brand-new day.

Stay within this moment for the miracle is here

There's nothing that you need to do, nothing but be sincere

Life is bursting forth in every breath; And in the stillness find

A place to love, a place to join with every heart and mind.

Rejoice, for in this moment you can send blessings near and far

Rejoice, for in this moment you are a living star

And every time you feel afraid and wonder what to do

Come back to this one moment and know the miracle is you.

Appendix C

A Teacher, A Mentor, A Friend

This letter is written to Davida Hoyos, my devoted friend for over two decades.

Davida, *if you only knew...*

Today is August 11th and if you were still alive today, this would be your birthday. And more than likely, we would be celebrating it in the one of the many ways that you love to celebrate. You were the "quintessential Leo." You loved bravado, good taste and a good party!

One of my favourite parties was when you asked everyone to bring you something that represented something we loved.

I made you the Cat Jam Jazz/Blues Band set on a two-tiered cardboard box that I painted purple. It was equipped with a mirrored dance floor with dancers and musicians—all cats, of course—and made with pipe cleaners and it was the most fun project I had ever worked on! I mean, it did represent things I loved and continue to love—music, dance, and cats!

And how I loved you for as long as our friendship was alive… and still.

So many things I wanted to tell you. I hope you can hear me now.

What was buried so deeply in a protective bolder so that I wouldn't shatter into rock, then crumble into sand, erupted last night in a shocking blast of dynamite.

There is no protective cover now—I come to you raw—my soul fully exposed… and in memory I see you there when you opened your door as you had for two decades of our lives always dressed to the nines—larger than life—all 5 foot ten of you and your wild flaming red hair and our hugs which sometimes felt more like visits, just as often got cut short by the excitement of what we were about to share…. the latest news coupled with gossip and giggles, disappointments and tears as we cared and we shared and paired as no other in our lives at that time. And even with daily visits when we lived in the same building or the most—weekly visits when we didn't', we came to each other brand new every time.

And then the day came that I dreaded, the day I had to tell you my news that I was moving to the west coast—to the place my soul longed to be for 30 years—and I watched as your face went pale as you attempted a smile and told me how happy you were for me. And although you may have been, it was just too hard for you…not again…not again…too many endings to bear.

You couldn't stand the pain of another person you loved leaving you. You chose your few friends carefully and with any perceived threat you would leave them before they could leave you. So you withdrew from me…and then withdrew even more and you built walls to protect your heart which left my heart broken so deep in despair that eventually I copied you and built my own walls to cover a loss that no words could comfort.

And then Carla's call one week ago. 5:30 in the morning. Sorry to wake you. June, but I knew you would want to know. Davida died yesterday morning. And I shrieked NO! And I hung up the phone with tears streaming down my face and grabbed my journal and madly scribbled twenty-two pages of heartbreak. But it wasn't enough—there was more. I was driven now, the dam had burst. The rock was now sand and before it was swallowed by the sea, I had to embody it all. You, me, us… So I found the file that carried the remnants of our life—almost too heavy to carry filled with all the cards and letters and poetry and paintings that I could never throw out and even though it split my heart open to be with all these memories that spoke our story of love—a love that was supposed to last forever no matter where our geography took us, I needed to remember every one. I needed to get drunk on your essence. So what I always wanted to tell you Davida is this: I have always missed you and I do still.

So here we are meeting again. a meeting beyond the veil. But it's a transparent veil and I can see your eyes. I can almost touch you.

You know, I looked at your painting the other night before I went to bed. It has been hanging on my wall since I moved here three years ago and has hung in every home I've ever lived since you gave it to me for my fortieth birthday—twenty-one years after we met. And I looked at it that night as though I was looking at it for the very first time…and it was curious. I wondered if I should still keep it there. Maybe I should take it down. After all, you weren't in my life any more. The friendship was long over. But as I stood there taking in the brilliant colours of every flower on the canvas, so vivid you could almost smell their fragrance and the monarch butterfly finding its' nectar in the calla lily, a sadness washed over me…but also a love so pure that I knew I couldn't and I wouldn't take it down.

We haven't spoken in about four years—no it's probably been seven or eight, but I want to lie… I want to believe that it never happened at all. That we spoke every day. That you did wish me well, that you withstood the geographical distance between us and you changed your adamant refusal to use email and so we would, and we'd talk on the phone and you'd come to visit me and I'd show you what drew me to this wonderous land and I'd make you my first priority on every return to Toronto. And we'd still be holding hands across the miles…to this very day…or at least 'til the day you died. And now you left me. You left me! As long as I knew you were alive, there was always a tinge of hope that we'd find our way back to one another. You were not just my friend, you were my mentor. I could never repay you for what you taught me.

I was only twenty-eight. You were thirty when we met in Montreal and I have to admit I was intimidated by you. Intimidated by your worldliness, your stately beauty, self-assurance, intellect, sophistication, passion for theatre and painting and Judaism and your poetry…oh yes, your poetry…which is what bound us together in the first place. We began to meet regularly and read each other our poetry. Mine always felt insignificant compared to yours. Yours were filled with stunning imagery, metaphor, never superfluous. You used words I had never heard of but I knew what they meant because my heart understood.

And somehow my poetry moved you...or perhaps it was my ability to be vulnerable and opening my heart on the page, not in a sophisticated way, but in a real way that made you love me. Your poetry became your medicine as you blasted through your world in a flurry of activity, at the hub of the Montreal's largest cultural events.

You immersed yourself so completely so you wouldn't feel the unspeakable loss of Leo's death. It happened only a year before I met you but it took months before you told me the details. Until then you assumed the Jacqueline Kennedy stance of holding your head high, dignified. You put a padlock on the part of your heart that died the day that he did.

There you were, on vacation in Mexico with your best friends, celebrating your 6th anniversary when suddenly he keeled over on the dance floor and was dead by the time he hit the ground. A brain aneurysm. Six months later your other beloved best friend died, your father. The man you worshipped. The man who taught you the richness of life. The one with whom you shared Torah and philosophy and literature and politics. The one who instilled in you a love and thirst for knowledge where learning became as essential as breathing. And you brought this learning to your students for thirty years.

Davida's Place, Where Learning Is Fun. Your private tutorial and remediation academy. The place for kids to come after school to work on the subjects they couldn't pass. The students that the teachers and parents and psychologists believed would never know academic achievement having failed year after year. But not you. You threw away all the so-called professional reports and found the soul of every child and loved them back to life. Little by little they began to stand taller and their grades improved until they aced them and went on to university. That wasn't a one-time deal. That was the norm. And it wasn't just the kids. It was me too. Without your encouragement, love, mentorship and tutelage, I would never have gone back to school. You saw my intelligence and ability when I could not. You told me I was an excellent writer when you read my papers and you were not one to compliment when it came to academics unless it was deserved. And you guided me to the halls of York University and your joy was unsurpassed with each of my successes.

It was during that time we lived in the same apartment building. We would often spend our Saturday or Sunday nights playing scrabble, listening to Leonard Cohen, Laura Nyro, Janis Ian, Carol King, The Beatles, Joni Mitchel and filling the ashtray with cigarette after cigarette. On one such occasion, I was in one of my depressed states and felt unsafe going down the stairwell to my apartment after midnight and asked if you would walk me down. You looked at me with my hair in curlers, my pink rabbit pyjamas with the bunny ears hood and remarked with a straight face and meaning every word, "June, you are singularly unattractive. You needn't worry." That cracked me up and I went skipping down the stairs. I loved your humour. In fact, I loved and cherished everything about you.

Even after you told me that our friendship was over and to please stop calling you, I couldn't. So I sent you a video of my play, *Madness, Masks and Miracles* and you wrote me a letter that praised the writing, the performance, the brilliance of it, and your words meant more to me than any of the other accolades I received.

So Davida, if you were here, and of course you are, with all my heart I thank you. I thank you for the hugs and the love and scrabble games and the picnics and camping trips and the Passover seder dinners and oh my gosh…I could go on forever, couldn't I?

And here you are right now beside me. Just as you were the night I stood and looked at your painting. You came to tell me all is forgiven and that you always loved me too.

You came to tell me you are at peace…and there is nothing that I would ever want more for you. I love you, my forever friend.

Shalom.

Baruch ha'shem.

Junie

Acknowledgments

I am indeed privileged and have often said that if everyone was as supported as much as I am, there would be no shortage of joy on the planet. This may sound verbose, but it is not. I am blessed with family, friends, students, clients, teachers, mentors, and coaches who love and care about me, as well as my loving partner, David Halliwell, who champions every one of my successes. His own creativity and kindness inspire me to continue walking the high road of life and count my blessings over and over again. I have not always been well enough to recognize the enormity of love with which I have been blessed.

A story that comes to mind is when I was forty-nine years old and decided to move alone with my cats three thousand miles across the country to Vancouver from Toronto. I knew only two people on the West Coast and only casually but had been drawn to the ocean and mountains and the way they made me feel from the first time I hitched there as a young hippy in 1970. I was about to start all over and hoped I would find a community of friends.

Over my lifetime, I had accumulated hundreds of cards, letters, and mementos, including matchboxes and swizzle sticks, that I threw in an old trunk. I decided to go through that trunk before leaving Toronto because I didn't want to take it with me. I gave myself six months. I carefully read the postcards and letters—many of them love letters, some from people I didn't remember. Then, when I was finished, and just days before setting out on my journey, I took them to my friend's cottage and had a fire ceremony. I burned each one and blessed each person who took the time, energy, and love to share with me a part of his or her life. It was then that I realized all the love I have always had throughout my life, yet so often I felt alone and lonely. I decided that on this next adventure, I would stay awake to the love I was receiving and know, too, I am never alone.

To all of you whose path has crossed my own—I thank you. You are the reason I am who I am. Just like I said in the dedication, there are those who came bearing gifts of flowers and some with two-by-fours. The vast majority of you have gifted me with a stunning garden that will bloom in my heart forever. |One such person is Manny Myer—a man with a golden heart. Manny seems to love everyone unconditionally. Upon learning I was about to write another book, he purchased the desk upon which I wrote it as a simple expression of loving kindness. And it is this energy that I aspired to embody onto these pages—born of seeds of loving kindness from our collaborative garden. May my words nourish and bless your heart and soul as you have done mine.

Someone else I wish to thank by name is Dr. Angela E. Lauria, founder of The Author Incubator. You have indeed stretched me as a writer and an author with your brilliant system, The Author's Way. As a writing coach, I know what it feels like to support writers on their writing path—but I myself have never known this kind of loving support that you and your team so generously and enthusiastically have given. Thank you so much.

Last but not least, thank you to David Hancock and the Morgan James Publishing team for helping me bring this book to print.

Love,

Junie

Thank You

To you, my honoured reader, I extend my heartfelt thanks as you continue on the courageous journey of giving your treasured story a new life through the written word. I am overjoyed that I've been able to offer the steppingstones of writing your life's story, and I am eager to continue this journey with you! As a special gift to you, I am offering a free class to enhance your memoir writing experience. Please contact me at junie@junieswadron.com to receive this gift.

If you find you would like even further guidance to keep you walking this triumphant path, I am available to assist you. No matter where you are in the process of finishing your book or finding your voice for podcasts, stages, or facilitating groups and online programs, I am happy to continue coaching you. It is a privilege and an honour. You can stay in touch with my current courses, workshops, and writing retreats at www.junieswadron.com. You can reach me personally at junie@junieswadron.com. Thank you for believing in your story and knowing that your life matters!

About the Author

Junie Swadron is an author, psychotherapist, international speaker, workshop facilitator, and professional writing coach who has spent the last twenty-five years guiding thousands of students in writing and sharing their life stories.

Junie sees the therapeutic process and the creative process as one. It is about accessing a special place within us where serenity, love, courage, and truth reside. It is from this place where we begin to know our true spirit. It is from this place we begin to heal.

What makes Junie an extraordinary healer is that she knows "both sides of the couch." She was diagnosed with manic-depressive illness at age twenty and has lived with its challenges for more than thirty years. Her personal experiences have taught her resiliency and coping strategies for choosing health and wellness again and again. Junie has the natural gift of feeling another's joy and pain inside of her own body. She has always shown sincere interest and listens with reverence when people share their sacred stories with her. She considers it an honour and a privilege.

Junie Swadron is known for helping people honour the journeys they have walked, the unique paths that have led them to who they are today. She is fascinated by the stories that make up a person's life. And even though you've never met, she is sincere when she asks, "What's your story?"